STEPPING

St🪨nes

to Business Success

200 Tips on How to Succeed in Business

Book 1 of the Stepping Stones Series

Donna Stone

BALBOA.
PRESS

A DIVISION OF HAY HOUSE

Balboa Press books may be ordered through booksellers or by contacting:

Balboa Press
A Division of Hay House
1663 Liberty Drive
Bloomington, IN 47403
www.balboapress.com.au
1-(877) 407-4847

ISBN: 978-1-4525-0913-6 (sc)
ISBN: 978-1-4525-0914-3 (e)

Because of the dynamic nature of the Internet, any web addresses or links contained in this book may have changed since publication and may no longer be valid. The views expressed in this work are solely those of the author and do not necessarily reflect the views of the publisher, and the publisher hereby disclaims any responsibility for them.

All care has been taken in compiling the contents of this book, but no guarantees are given in relation to its accuracy. This book represents the opinions of the author only and the information in this book has been obtained by the author solely from her own experiences as a Bookkeeper and is provided as general information only.

No reader should rely solely on the information contained in this publication as it does not purport to be comprehensive or to render specific advice. As such it is not intended for use as a source of investment or business advice. All readers are advised to retain competent counsel from legal and accounting advisers to determine their own specific business needs.

The author and publisher expressly disclaim all and any liability to any person, whether or not the purchaser of this publication, in respect of anything and of the consequences of anything done or omitted to be done by any such person in reliance, whether whole or partial, upon the whole or any part of the contents of this publication.

Any people depicted in stock imagery provided by Thinkstock are models, and such images are being used for illustrative purposes only.
Certain stock imagery © Thinkstock.

Printed in the United States of America

Balboa Press rev. date: 04/16/2013

Contents

Dedication

This book is dedicated to the three most important men in my life; my sons. To Matthew, Daniel and Nathan—I am so rich for having you all in my life. I am honoured to call myself your mum.

Love you guys! ☺ Mum.

MONEY GEM STONES

Grow Your Business the Easy Way

Free Business Education
at
www.blackbeltbusiness.com.au

Introduction & Welcome

Firstly, thank you for selecting and buying this book. Whilst this is my first book, I am certainly not new to writing or to being published, with dozens and dozens of articles published in My Business Magazine as well as Women's Networking Association Magazine, CEO Online and more. If you have seen these articles you may recognise some familiar content, but of course I have included heaps of new and fresh material.

You can read this book in two ways. Either scan the tip headers and then read only the pieces which interest you at present or simply read from cover to cover. I hope you will choose at some point the latter, as I strongly believe there is heaps of practical information in this book. Some things you may know, some will be a good refresher and some information will be totally new to you.

Why should you spend your valuable time reading my book? What is my claim to be an authority on business? Well, my background covers a range of areas, but most notably I have over 25 years experience in bookkeeping. I have completed a number of formal studies and have also run a private employment agency and have worked in both legal firms and Chartered Accountants. Most importantly, I have run my own successful small business now for over 10 years. I started small, with just myself and one part-time staff member, and grew to having a team of over 12 staff. Like many of you, I have had to wear all of the hats at one time (marketer, bookkeeper, staff supervisor, advertiser, debt collector and technician) and then have gone through the steps of growth to a point where I have team members who wear each of those different hats. Been there, done that.

So, find a comfortable chair, grab a coffee and sit back. Feel free to write notes in the margin, use a coloured highlighter pen to emphasise important points or put post-it tags on pages you wish to revisit. This book should be used, not kept in pristine condition and stuck on a shelf. In fact I believe only 10% of books purchased are actually read—so I hope this book does NOT become one of those statistics. I sincerely hope you enjoy this book, find some valuable pointers and establish a business that is both successful and fulfilling to you. Wishing you all the very best with your business.

Donna

March 2011

Testimonials

Great practical "how-to" tips for the small business world, presented in a very reader friendly format.
—Colleen Tarrant, CPD Accountants

Donna Stone's bright, heartfelt writing makes business seem like fun, but also conveys useful information that will remind anyone in business of the fundamentals that make a profitable difference.
—Simon Sharwood, Editor, My Business Magazine

Insightful and focused, but most importantly it's totally practical! You can be certain that Donna is speaking from absolute experience when she dishes up all these little 'gems' that you can and should use right now in your business.
—Glenn Walford, Author of 'Shaking the Profit' Series

We laugh off the common sense behind business activities, engagements and it's refreshing to receive insight and real experience answers. Donna Stone easily relays and addresses the crux of business from her exposure to real Australian business's and makes your and my next stepping stones in business conscious. Thank you for making our business and team actively engaged in business life.
—Andrea Blunden, Gretchen Operations Captain

Finally! A business book that has it all. You'll find yourself shaking you head in disbelief on how easy it is for business success. This book, or Business Bible, is for all levels of business owners and managers. It will save you and your business time and money. I educate business owners everyday and now have a secret weapon. Stepping Stones to Business Success is a must for all business owners and managers.
—Nathan McDonald, Black Belt Business

A must read for anyone in small business. Donna offers practical no-nonsense solutions for many of the challenges faced by business owners today, drawing on her own wealth of wisdom and experience. If you want to succeed in business you need Stepping Stones to Business Success!

—Karen Phillips, Direct Office Products

Donna has written a fantastic guide of tried and tested tips to success, you can sense the experience she has been through in each and every one of them. All businesses, no matter what stage they are at, would benefit from reading this book and keeping it close by.

—Anita Plath, President
—Redland City Chamber of Commerce

It's the straight talking business handbook of the year and every budding entrepreneur needs to own it. Without doubt—what you don't know about business will hurt you. But armed with this comprehensive and down to earth game plan—small business success becomes like second nature.

—Lynette L Palming AM, Founder and
Managing Director Women's Network Australia

This book is an absolute must read for anyone wanting to succeed in business and enjoy life while doing it. Donna Stone is proof that 'a challenge is an opportunity in disguise.' She is a remarkable businesswoman who embodies the personal characteristics of strength, courage and commitment.

—Kay Danes, International Bestselling Author

There's a saying "Commonsense ain't common". That saying also applies to business. Donna's book provides the information and knowledge that you can apply to your business. So read it and apply it.

—John Sciacca, Director/Accountant,
Sciacca Salomone Accountants

Donna is a very experienced business owner and has great business success information to share. Her knowledge in so many areas of business is shared in many of her other publications plus this book. I highly recommend this great read.

—Julie & Doug Bannister
—Key Business Network

Stepping Stones to Business Success is a great resource tool for any business owner. I'm often heard saying, "You don't have to implement a thousand things to make a difference in your business. Just implementing two or three things can make a big difference to the bottom line." This book gives you practical ways on how you can start to improve your business.

—Mal Emery Australia's Millionaire Maker
—www.MalEmery.com

Bookkeeping & Accounting

"Small differences in your performance can lead to large differences in your results."

—Brian Tracy (Motivational Coach)

INTRODUCTION TO BOOKKEEPING & ACCOUNTING

Until you, as a business owner or operator, can fully appreciate the importance of knowing your figures, the value of quality bookkeeping and the worth of being informed on your business' financial performance, I honestly do not believe your business can move to the next level. I am not saying do it all yourself, quite the opposite, but you do need to know your figures. The expression used to be "CASH IS KING" . . . now it's "CASH IS THE WHOLE ROYAL FAMILY".

 Ratios & Key Performance Indicators— Ratios

Bookkeeping & Accounting

Key Performance Indicators (KPI's) are great tools. If you work with a business coach for example, they will definitely introduce these to you, as a critical part of running your business, and it does not have to be time consuming. And of course most franchise systems will have a set of KPI's specific to their business model. I have my own KPI's in a one page Excel spreadsheet, all listed down the side. Then across the top, I break it up into each month, which is excellent because at a single glance I can see, in simple terms, how my business is performing. Here are a couple of very simple performance indicators, and obviously each business is different. A high stock business will put emphasis on different indicators, than for example, a service-based business.

There are a string of handy little ratios, which are simple and easy to calculate. The first I would suggest is Net Profit as a % of Sales.

Let's say that your sales last month were $285,000 and your net profit (bottom line) was $11,800. See below:

11800 ÷ 285000 x 1/100. ANSWER: 4.14%

Some other excellent ratios (usually calculated via a process similar to the above) are:

- Debtors as a % of Sales
- Direct Costs (COGS) as a % of Sales
- Overheads as a % of Sales
- Wages as a % of Sales (and you might want to include super in these figures)

2 Ratios & Key Performance Indicators— Average Sale Value

Bookkeeping & Accounting

Simply take the total income for the month and divide by number of sales. Let's use the $285,000 above and say the number of sales was 159. ANSWER: $1792. Now, remember that if you want to determine number of sales (i.e. transactions) or average customer sale, the calculations are very similar. If you invoiced 85 customers that month, then average customer value would be $285,000 ÷ 85. ANSWER: $3353. Be sure to be consistent. If you are using EX GST figures, then do this every month.

TIP: I would use figures exclusive of GST as this is what is posted to your profit and loss (P&L) statement. When you make a sale of $110 including GST, $100 goes to sales and $10 goes to the balance sheet as "GST on Sales" and a liability account, as you will have to remit this money to the ATO on your next BAS.

3

Ratios & Key Performance Indicators— Calculating Average Collection Days

This one is really important and rarely calculated. If it is taking you 105 days on average to get paid, guess what, the "life blood" of your business is being choked off. And it is a statistical fact, that the longer you let a debt go outstanding, the greater the likelihood you will not recoup that debt. Set yourself a goal to reduce the average collection days by at least one day EVERY month from now on—you will be amazed at how much stronger your business will become. Heard the phase "cash is king"? Well there is a new phrase "Cash is the whole royal family".

A = sales for the last 12 months (inc GST, let's use $3,762,000)
B = days in the year (let's use 365)
C = debtors value for the last month (in this example, let's use $270,000

$$\frac{A}{B} = X \quad \text{then} \quad \frac{C}{X} = Y$$

$$\frac{3762000}{365} = 10,307 \quad \text{then} \quad \frac{270000}{10307} = 26.2$$

ANSWER: In this scenario, it takes the business on average 26.2 days to collect their debts.

Here is another tip. I do step one, once a year. Then each month I do step two in an Excel spreadsheet where I have the formula already set up. Let's say in cell C14 I have keyed in my month end debtors (in this example $270,000). I already know from doing step one previously that X = 10,307. In the appropriate cell in my monthly spreadsheet, I have entered the formula: =C14/10307 so the calculation is automatic, simple and easy.

4 Ratios & Key Performance Indicators— Working out Enquiry Conversion Cost

Work out your cost per annum to gain a new client. Include advertising costs, networking costs, printing of business cards and general promotion. Say it's $30,000 per annum, which equates to $2500 per month. If you invoice 3 new clients this month, then your enquiry conversion cost is: 2500 ÷ 3 = $833. This is the cost it takes you to gain that client. Usually it costs more to gain a new client than to keep an existing client, so this reminds us to value our good clients and look after them!

5 Ratios & Key Performance Indicators— Conversion Percent on Leads

This is another good one. Every business should be tracking where their leads come from. So, by tracking your leads you know, for example, you had 15 leads this month. If you had 3 new clients, your conversion percentage would equate to 20%. This means of course, if you wanted to get 5 new clients next month, you would need 25 leads! (25 x 20% = 5).

Please do not be daunted by the calculations. I am sure a whole bunch of people switched off completely as soon as they saw some figures and basic formulas! These are straight-forward calculations and most of them will apply to most businesses, regardless of the type of business you are operating. You may already track and monitor some of these indicators but I know from experience that many business owners simply don't.

Bookkeeping & Accounting

Well, the word now is not that "cash is king" but that now "cash is the whole royal family!" Cash is crucial to keeping any business running; if your cash tightens up, you may as well have severed your carotid artery. So, here are **21** really practical and down to earth points for businesses to keep their cash flowing.

- Invoice immediately or frequently. If you do larger projects, be sure to invoice in instalments (progress claims) but otherwise invoice immediately after the job, or at least weekly. You need to invoice to get paid.
- Make it easy for a client to pay. Include your bank details on the invoice and have various options for payment, such as, direct, BPAY, Credit Card or cheque.
- Debt collect every week. Yes—weekly! Have a system, a schedule and keep notes. When someone makes a promise but fails to fulfil, follow up as you should have noted all promises and when they were made. Remember the adage "the squeaky wheel gets the grease". Squeak heaps and get those payments in quicker. It is a statistical fact that the longer you let an account go unpaid, the more likelihood of you not being paid—at all.
- Know your margins and your cycles, and of course, keep your bookkeeping up to date. A sale may mean income (in the books) but the reality is that it's when the client pays that's critical. If your average collection days are say 70 and you are buying lots of stock, which has to be paid in 30 days, you are carrying a lot in debtors, as money owing to you. Try to close the gap. If you can buy on credit 30 days from end of month, buy early in the month so you essentially get up to 60 days. Cut the debtors from 70 to 50 days and you will be ahead.

- Keep stock purchases to a minimum—do not carry any more stock than necessary. Of course you have to have stock to keep the business going, but know what moves and what does not. For example, I am a MYOB software re-seller. Some levels sell heaps and I stock these, but other levels (the very high levels) move slowly so I order these in on a needs-only basis.
- Have client/customer agreements and be sure to cover aspects such as interest or fees you charge on late payments—remember you are not a free bank for your customers; if you owe the ATO money, they have a GIC (general interest charge) why shouldn't you?
- Get customers/clients to pay deposits on work—especially if you have stock. It is quite common for businesses with high value stock items (such as cabinet makers) to ask for a 30% deposit.
- Do not release work until you are paid. Many service-orientated businesses, will not release work (e.g. Accountants with clients tax returns) until they are paid, or at least the old account is settled.
- If you have a client who has a bad history of payment or looks to be going bankrupt, then definitely work on a pre-payment system. With a bad history, it is very fair to ask for prepayment in order to keep doing their work.
- Consider "sacking" the "D" grade clients. If they are hard work, always unjustly complain and then do not pay—you do not want them. Honestly. Move them out to make room for a new "A" grade client.
- Look after your "A" and "B" grade clients. These are great clients and you value them, so be sure to look after them and not put so much emphasis on gaining new clients that you neglect the old. Find at least one thing you can value add to these clients (perhaps a free report, or additional free service) to show thanks for their custom.
- If you have a new client who has no history with you, again work on a pre-payment system for 3-6 months. Be

polite and explain it is standard Corporate Policy—most (especially if they have good payment intentions) will understand and be okay with that.

- Do not discount. Look at a "discounting table" on the internet—it really can be scary. You will see for example that if your gross profit margin is say 15% and you discount by a tiny 5%, then you actually need to double your sales volume to achieve the same gross profit.
- Ask suppliers for early payment discounts. Although you know discounting isn't good, it doesn't mean you can't ask your suppliers for discounts if you pay early. They may decide that having the payment early is worth giving out the discount.
- Watch your expenses. Ensure you are not paying a fortune in phone services, or bank fees, but don't be silly about it. Remember you "need to spend money to make money". Do not cut costs on things like marketing and advertising as these costs are really investments in your business and critical to its good health.
- Ensure your marketing/advertising is working. Above I said to not cut costs, but be sure you spend well. Track your leads. Ask every new enquiry how they heard about you and write it down. If you spend money on an advert that generates zero enquiries, then it's close to wasted money.
- Review/revamp your website. We are in the age of technology and most people search via the internet. When did you last review your website? Or gosh, do you even have one? For most businesses, an effective website can really generate a lot of work. Use it.
- Secure the services of a good accountant—this will help (legally) with tax liabilities and possibly reduce the need for instalment, and thus free your cash up further.
- See your solicitor or accountant regarding your entity setup. Not only is the setup critical for asset protection, but quite often you can (legally) pay less tax with the correct setup. For example, why pay individual tax at 46.5%, rather than corporate tax at 30%?

- Engage a mentor or business coach. Often (especially those of us in small business) we can benefit from advice from a coach or mentor. Maybe we just need someone to keep us focussed and on track, or to ask curly questions. Do not forget your accountant here too—a good one will help your business with more than just tax return preparation.
- Educate yourself—read articles on business subjects, attend seminars and gain knowledge. Sometimes it is not only about learning something new, but refreshing ourselves with reminders on what we should be doing—and then **do it.**

7 Ensure you are Set up Properly

Bookkeeping & Accounting

There are various entity setups which each have their own pros and cons. It is best you see your accountant or solicitor to ensure the best setup for you, but here is a brief table to give you an idea of some advantages and disadvantages of some of the basic structures:

Setup	Advantages	Disadvantages
Sole Trader	• Simple form of setup • Little setup cost • Cheap to run	• Limited protection • No asset protection • No tax benefit
Partnership	• Cheap setup cost • Cheap ongoing costs • Suits husband/wife	• Partners can incur debt • Needs restructure at each change of partners
Company	• Asset protection • Max tax at 30% • Limited liability	• Expensive to set up • Directors responsibilities • Director loans unwise
Trust	• Asset protection • Less expensive than Coy	• All profits have to be distributed to beneficiaries

8 Bookkeeping is an Essential Part of your Business

Having been a bookkeeper for over 25 years, I have experienced a lot. So many businesses have no idea how important good bookkeeping is. In a recent CPA survey, it was found that 5% of businesses never do bank reconciliations. I have heard phrases like "I don't have time" or "it's not important—my bookkeeping can wait till later". If your bookkeeper (or bookkeeping) is three months behind, you have little idea of how you are going now, and will not until three months time. If you are twelve months behind, how do you have any idea of how you are faring? You might be operating insolvent and not even have a clue. How can you make informed decisions about your business? How will you know your wage ratios have increased if you do not have accurate (and up to date) records? It is a statistical fact: **5% of business failures are due to poor (or absent) bookkeeping.** There are other reasons that a business fails, some of which might be out of your control, but your bookkeeping is one of the things that is in your control. Anyone who has succeeded in business will say they are always on top of their bookwork. Examples of where accurate and timely bookkeeping is important:

- Debt Collection—how can you collect what is owing to you if you do not know what is owing?
- Cashflow—if you do not invoice, the money is going to dry up pretty quickly.
- Business Decisions—how can you curb your spending if you do not know how much you have spent or how your business is actually going? How can a coach guide you if the figures are not there?
- Finance & Banks—if you go for finance, you will have to provide figures and tax returns
- GST & BAS—these have to be done, often quarterly, and must be done right

- Selling—if you are going to sell your business, then this is critical; it is one of the first things a prospective buyer will look at.

Business owners must be monitoring their reports, at the very least a monthly Profit & Loss report, but ideally a multi-period version, which shows you the current month as well as prior months, so you can see where you are heading. Depending on the business, you may review other reports, including payroll costs, stock, balance sheets and inventory reports. After all, if you do not know exactly where you have come from, how can you have an idea of where you are heading?

 How to Find a good Accountant

Bookkeeping & Accounting

- How did you find your accountant? Were they simply geographically handy or more importantly were they referred to you? Was the person who referred them to you, someone you admire as a successful person in business?
- Do you feel comfortable talking to him/her?
- Does he or she talk in easy to understand English?
- Does your accountant do more than just your tax return? Does he or she cover business advice?
- Is he or she qualified and a member of a professional body? If you have your tax done by a budget tax firm, for example one that advertises, 'Tax Returns for $79' then don't expect anything more than getting a basic tax return done. You will unlikely get business advice, financial advice, tax planning or tax advice. It's the bare tax return and rarely more.
- Are they technically competent?
- Are they able to listen and to not appear rushed?
- Are they accessible? Can you speak to or meet with them?

- Are they pro-active or reactive? Do they regularly see you?
- Are they flexible with regard to changing trends? → E.g. do they use a computer?!!!
- Are they honest, reliable and have integrity? Does he or she keep promises made?

10 Things to Consider When Choosing a Bookkeeper

Bookkeeping & Accounting

- Does your bookkeeper keep you on task?
- Does your bookkeeper offer advice?
- Does your bookkeeper treat you with respect?
- Does your bookkeeper keep you informed?
- Is your bookkeeper a single operator or part of a team?

Here are a couple of questions to ask yourself:

- How did you find your bookkeeper? If your accountant or a friend in business recommended them, this is a good sign. A recommendation is one of the best ways of knowing someone else uses this service and is happy with it.
- Does your bookkeeper ask for paperwork? Most of our new clients ask me why I want to see their vehicle registration paperwork or their electricity account . . . "my old bookkeeper never asked me for this info" . . . We like to be thorough in order to do our job properly. If you do not get asked for this stuff, things are not being recorded properly.
- Does your bookkeeper ask questions (intelligent ones, of course)? A good bookkeeper does not guess or assume or presume everything, unless it's quite obvious. If you do not write something on your chequebook butt, then they should

be quizzing you about this. Remember what ASSUME stands for—"making an ASS out of U and ME".

- Does your accountant complain about the standard of your books? If they do, there is probably a problem here.
- Is your bookkeeper qualified or at least a member of a professional body? If they are a member of a professional body they are more likely to have to do further education, which means keeping up to date with rules and regulations. Does your bookkeeper participate in further training? Do they attend ATO Satellite seminars for example?
- Does your bookkeeper have multiple clients? If they have only one or two clients, then most likely it is a "backyard" operation and of course you are not getting the expertise developed from multiple client dealings.
- Does your bookkeeper operate in a professional way? Whilst a bookkeeper may be operating as a home-based business, this does not mean your bookkeeping has to be done on the kitchen table. Many home-based businesses are extremely professional and successful—the question is, how professional is your bookkeeper? Everything from how they answer their phone, to their equipment, office, report presentation to their website, email signature etc. In fact, a home-based business is usually good news for you—they do not have rental expenses, so less overhead costs should mean savings to you, their client.
- Is your bookkeeper a single operator or part of a team? This can be a critical one for you. Let's say it is a week before the BAS is due and your bookkeeper is sick . . . if they are a single operator, and seriously sick, then it is likely your work just will not get done. If the bookkeeping business you deal with has multiple staff, then if one person is sick (or leaves for that matter) then it should be a fairly seamless transition of your books to another member of the team (whether permanent or temporary) and your business does not suffer.

- If your bookkeeper is part of a team, do you get the same person each month handling your books, or is the bookkeeping business having such a high turnover of staff, that it is a different person every time?
- Does your bookkeeper liaise with your accountant a reasonable amount of the time? Is your bookkeeper comfortable asking questions or bringing things to his/her attention? Communication is another important aspect of helping you to run your business. Remember two heads are better than one and asking the accountant an occasional question, or giving them information can only be beneficial for your business.
- Does your bookkeeper keep you informed? Do you get weekly, or monthly or at least quarterly reports? Can you ask a question and get a fairly prompt response? Again, is communication open?
- Does your bookkeeper offer advice? Do they give suggestions on how to improve things or do things better or how to fix problems? Or if not how, can they direct you to someone who can? Good bookkeeping should be more than just "plugging in the figures" . . . it should be helping you to improve your business.
- Does your bookkeeper keep you on task? Do they ensure your compliance deadlines (BAS, tax etc) are met on time? Without feeling you are being harassed, does your bookkeeper keep prompting you so that deadlines are met? Are you constantly getting late fees and you know it is not because you are holding out on information after being prompted?
- Does your bookkeeper (or MYOB consultant/trainer) treat you with respect? Are they friendly and polite? Do not tolerate bossy, grumpy or condescending bookkeepers or trainers. Remember, it is YOUR business, you are the boss. You should feel comfortable with the person you are dealing with.

In the 2008 CPA Small Business Survey, it was found that a whopping 44% of small businesses do not produce a debtors report!! And just as bad, 25% of small businesses never chase up late payments. Interestingly the same survey for 2009 and 2010 still have 25% of small businesses never chasing payment. A healthy and smart business will produce debtor (receivable) reports every week and chase those outstanding every week. But first, it is important that you invoice promptly, have an Agreement in place and ring every week. When you call (and ring, don't just email or post out an overdue reminder statement or notice), be sure to note promises etc, so when you call back (and do call back if required) you can quote a promise which will further help you to get the money in. Have a person doing this who is professional and friendly but firm. They do not have to be a "pit bull" but someone who will do the job properly.

Have a process in place, where in the case a promise is not met, or the debtor skilfully avoids your calls, you have a set "Collection Letter". This letter should be firm although polite. Tell them what they owe and when you want it paid and what the consequence will be if they do not do this—that is, the matter will go to your solicitor or debt collection agency for action and they may be liable for the costs associated with this. Have your process clearly in place so all your staff know what happens next, and when and why and how. Have a designated collection person. Not everyone likes or is able to do this; if you can give it to a person who is quite happy to do this task, all the better, they are likely to have more success than the person who absolutely hates this task. But if at the end of the day the person designated is not fond of collections, be sure to monitor their progress and ensure they are doing the job!

Be flexible. If your client owes $3K perhaps a repayment plan will be workable for them and will start getting that money in for you. Alternatively offering credit card facilities may help debtors pay.

It is my strong belief you need to train your clients and send the message that you are on top of payments. I can remember one client many years ago who said to me "Donna, I only pay you when you scream for it". So, I began "screaming" much sooner. Your clients will soon learn what you will accept or not and toe the line.

And, yes, you will lose some clients. I have had clients (amazingly usually those who were personal friends) who have been most indignant that I would even *ask* for payment. How dare I!! Well the fact remains, do you want a client or customer who does not pay for the service or product you have supplied? Those who are indignant at being asked for money should not be so rude as to put you in the position of *having* to ask. You do not need these clients; let them go to make room for those clients who will (happily) pay for your good service or product.

12 Increase your Rates or Prices Regularly

Bookkeeping & Accounting

I have known many businesses who were scared of increasing their prices. I will admit, I have been there myself in the beginning. The thing is, if you are providing a quality service or product, then you should increase your prices at regular intervals. If you do not, two things can happen:

- You start running at a loss and ultimately may have to fold
- You eventually do increase your prices, but because it has been maybe six years, it has got to be a whopper and it is too much for some clients or customers to swallow.

Increase your rates or prices regularly, perhaps every six months and no less than twelve monthly. Make it reasonable and fair and explain your reasons, for example, prices have gone up, or wage costs have increased. Be sure to give your clients/customers at least one full month's notice. If the increase is for example, $2/hour but this represents only a 4% increase, then say so, and especially point out that the CPI rate at present is say 4.25%.

Generally speaking, most clients (especially for service-based industries) will use a particular business because of the service they provide. If they perceive value for money, even if the rate is a little more than the next guy, then they do not mind. Look after your clients and customers and they will return to you.

13 Do not Discount; Instead Provide a Free Service or Value Add

Bookkeeping & Accounting

Have a look below. Let's imagine your margin is 30%. If you discount by 10%, then you have to work 50% harder (increase your sales volume by 50%) to achieve the same profit. Instead of discounting, offer some other incentive, such as value adding. A beautician may offer a free sample of a moisturiser with any facial. This has a dual purpose of also introducing the customer to another product, which they may like so much they may start using.

Discounting

If your present margin is

	20%	25%	30%	35%	40%	45%

And you reduce your price by:	To produce the same profits your sales volume must increase by:					
4%	25%	19%	15%	13%	11%	10%
8%	67%	47%	36%	30%	25%	22%
10%	100%	67%	50%	40%	33%	29%
12%	150%	92%	67%	52%	43%	36%
16%	400%	178%	114%	84%	67%	55%
20%	-	400%	200%	133%	100%	80%
25%	-	-	500%	250%	167%	125%
30%	-	-	-	600%	300%	200%

As you can see from the above table, it is actually very unwise to discount. To draw in business, consider instead value adding. Perhaps if a customer buys product "A" they get product "B" at either ½ price or even free. In particular, introducing a customer to a new product, which may generate recurring business, is even smarter. The customer feels they have received something for less, or nothing and so have got a good deal, and you still have your income. Remember too, a product you may sell for $20 may cost you $8, but even if it has cost you only $8 be sure the customer knows its full value.

In a service type business, you might actually offer a sample of another service you provide. This gives the client a free "taste" of your service and if they like what they '"taste" they may actually start using this extra service, which of course is extra business for you.

14

Business Theft & Fraud—
It Does Happen!

It is not only large faceless corporations that experience theft and fraud—every business can. Whether it is tools, or stock, money or time—we are all susceptible. In fact, possibly small business is more vulnerable because there are usually no checks and protective systems in place and one person is often doing many of the duties. Prevention does not have to be complicated or expensive or time consuming—it just requires some thought and pro-active attention to your business. "It won't happen to me" is the song so many of us sing with regard to theft, loss, accidents or anything that is particularly unpleasant. But the fact is that 80% of small business in Australia, during the business life, will be hit by employee theft or fraud with the median loss being $98,000. Analysts believe that internal theft is a primary cause of a large percentage of business failures.

Some examples of fraud I have personally experienced include:

- A bookkeeper sent letters to suppliers providing new bank details—hers! She raised lots of large sales credits so when payments went to her bank account the company debtors listing was not large. **AMOUNT STOLEN—UNKNOWN.**
- A bookkeeper paid fake invoices to fake suppliers—except bank details were her own and that of her husband. **AMOUNT STOLEN—$400,000 PLUS.**
- A bookkeeper made payments for real suppliers but instead of paying to their suppliers—the funds went to her bank account and she kept the statements and letters of demand and late notices hidden. **AMOUNT STOLEN—$100,000.**
- A bookkeeper had "ghost" employees. Some of the staff did not exist, but the money was going to her account. She

kept the amounts small and avoided detection for three years. **AMOUNT STOLEN—$87,000.**

- A bookkeeper collected cash from customers, wrote that the invoice was paid via Credit Card, but of course no credit card dockets were processed. Plus, if a supplier was owed say $600, she paid $1600, with $1K going to her own bank account. **AMOUNT STOLEN—$480,000 PLUS.**

15 Business Theft & Fraud—How to Avoid it

Bookkeeping & Accounting

Would you spend three hours a month to earn sales of $400,000? So why wouldn't you invest this time to avoid possibly substantial amounts being stolen! These are extremes which the diligent business owner will avoid with a little common sense and keeping in the know. Remember that the majority of bookkeepers and staff are basically very honest; however we should be prepared for the occasional "bad apple". Here are some tips on how to avoid business theft:

1. Have clear policies in place so staff know there will be no tolerance by the business of theft or fraud. Be transparent regarding the fact that you do have checks in place—so staff know things are being closely monitored. Lead by example and be honest in your dealings. If you steal, then how can you expect your staff to not follow your lead?
2. Rotate staff and their duties. Ensure your staff take regular annual leave. One client of mine, a camera retailer, discovered a dramatic improvement in their profit during the one month a suspect employee was on annual leave.
3. Have appropriate segregation of duties, such as, purchase versus payments. When one person does it all, then opportunities arise for dishonest staff to act. This can be

difficult for small businesses where there is only one or two staff, so you need to be careful in other ways.

4. Have a reconciliation process, cash register dockets etc. Ensure when you deal in cash (e.g. retail) that the banking reconciles to the till dockets or taking sheets.

5. Have suitable authorisation procedures for cheques, purchases etc.

6. Computer systems should be used by authorised personnel only with access controlled via methods such as password access. Does your system have "warning bells" such as credit limits being reached?

7. Ensure assets, inventory and stock are tracked and regular stock takes occur.

8. Conduct a random audit—even if informal. Watch bank movement. Trust your instincts or have an independent review by someone external and experienced, such as your accountant.

9. Have suitable reporting in place. Watch debtor and credit listings and other reports, such as Profit & Loss, Balance sheet etc. Review reports regularly.

10. Ensure your books are up to date; if they are not current how can you possibly find anomalies?

11. Be proactive—personally look at your books and bank statements. Trust your instincts (they are probably right) and ask questions. Do not allow your bookkeeper or staff member to make you feel guilty for asking questions. Any qualified, professional and honest bookkeeper or employee will encourage and support owner review.

12. If you seem to never have any cash, but the business appears to be doing very well—INVESTIGATE. It may be an error in the record keeping or an indicator that all is not well. Some ideas to consider:

  • liaise with your suppliers personally to check all is okay → account up to date?

  • look for large, or numerous sale credits in your books

- look for large, or numerous purchase credits in your books
- look for supplier names or employees you do not recognise.

16 Business Theft & Fraud—How to Detect It

Here are some tips on how to **detect** theft in your business. Each of these items on their own **does not** automatically correspond to theft occurring; they are just indicators—the majority of employees are honest; but you should keep your eyes open. General business indicators:

- Missing records or gaps in number sequences (i.e. dockets, orders or job/invoice numbers being skipped)
- Missing stock, inventory or merchandise
- Unlocked exits, especially at the back of the business
- A large number (dollar value or volume) of credits issued
- Your business takes in a fair amount of cash, but has virtually no reconciliations in place
- Financial reports are rarely provided—although an excuse is always provided
- You are working "like a dog", have heaps of work on, but just do not have any money
- Downturn in your bottom line (or change in ratios)—do not automatically blame the economy
- You are a business with a turnover of $1.2-2 million
- You have one office person handling purchasing, invoicing, receipting, banking and book work
- The business owner is so busy they do not have time to check things (and staff know this)
- The business owner is trusting; in fact they think of their staff as like their family.

Specific indicators about the staff member:

- Shows signs of alcohol or drug abuse (or is a gambler, which may be harder to detect)
- Displays abrupt changes in emotional behaviour
- Complains a lot (and often they are planning on leaving your employ)
- Defensive or hostile when asked about their work
- Says "sure" then you ask for something, but you never get that information
- Overly diligent, want to do everything, even tasks normally they would not need to
- Will not take holidays (because this is frequently when theft is discovered)
- Works long hours, especially outside normal business hours
- Puts things away when the owner enters the room; like they are hiding something
- Grabs the mail (as naturally they do not want others to see what's happening)
- Parks near exit doors (for easy access to steal stock out the back or side door)
- Appears to be living beyond their means.

It is believed that 25-40% of staff will steal at some point; it might be only a box of pens, or half a million dollars in cold, hard cash. If you feel something is not right, keep your eyes open, get financial reports (even if you have to learn the computer system to do so), and ask an independent party such as your accountant to review your figures and start checking things like your bank and credit card statements. If you spend an hour a week monitoring your business, checking your financial reports and being attentive, would this be worth saving $480K in theft? Discovery can be devastating; but not as devastating as watching your once thriving business going under.

Business Improvement

"Set higher standards for your own performance than anyone around you, and it won't matter whether you have a tough boss, or an easy one. It won't matter whether the competition is pushing you hard, because you'll be competing with yourself."

—Rick Pitino.

INTRODUCTION TO BUSINESS IMPROVEMENT

Well, as much as I hate to assume, it is probably a safe assumption that you want your business to improve. You want to learn and grow so that your business is a success on many levels. Hey, you purchased this book, so that is a great starting point.

17 Challenges

A challenge is an opportunity in disguise!

What a powerful statement and if you can live this philosophy, there will be no stopping you. Challenges test us, they also test our competitors who may quit because it is too hard. Challenges may force us to dig deeper or find a better way of doing something . . . which ultimately benefits and strengthens our business. I have always had a personal motto "What doesn't kill me only makes me stronger. Some days I feel like Arnold Schwarzenegger!" The same applies in business. Challenges are sent to us every day and it is how we address those challenges that make the difference. Do we quit? Do we whinge? Do we back down? Do we just decide it is all too hard and throw our arms up in the air?

We all know that opportunities are things to be grabbed, with both hands and held tightly. Every opportunity we are presented gives us the chance to do something wonderful with our business.

So, think of challenges as opportunities and accept them. You may not welcome them, but you definitely cannot shy away from them. Looking back in my own business, I can now see that every challenge I have accepted has resulted in a business improvement. Whether it was being time challenged and putting on my first team member Kate—I now have over a dozen wonderful team members—or being challenged by our computer system and discovering that networking was the solution. Take your challenges and use them as opportunities to do bigger and better things with your business.

18 Get a Great Attitude

Business Improvement

"You can't be a smart cookie if you have a crummy attitude".—John Maxwell.

Whether you are recruiting staff, or going out and promoting your business, it is all about attitude.

On the staff front, I strongly believe that it should be 80% attitude and 20% skill. If a person has the right attitude but is perhaps slightly lacking in skill, you know they can learn the skill. It is easy to teach the right person with a good attitude a new skill, but teaching someone to have the right attitude is a mighty lot of hard work—especially if they are not interested and really don't want to change their negative ways.

On a personal front, who gets promoted? It is the people who have positive attitudes, the 'can-do' philosophy and who get along with people. If you are a people person and have a positive attitude, you are more likely to exceed your peers when it comes to promotion.

So on a business front; doesn't it make sense that this same philosophy applies? Do you know of any (good) business coaches out there with a lousy attitude? Do people who have succeeded in business have a crummy attitude? I think not! They have the strong belief in their self, their team and their business that they will succeed. They know they are on track and have clear goals that are realizable. Positive psychological studies have shown that a positive and optimistic attitude can bring about better health and greater happiness. Let's face it, if you do not believe in yourself, or your staff or your business, then how can you possibly expect your prospective customers to have faith in you?

Attitude is contagious—if you have a great outlook and are positive, you attract positive outcomes, positive people will be more inclined to work with you and customers will believe you are the right choice to place their business with.

Following are some practical tips to having a positive attitude.

19 Get a Great Attitude—Lose the Negativity

Business Improvement

Do not talk negatively. For example, lately I have been flat out with work, but instead of putting a negative spin on it, and saying "it's been terribly busy", I have consciously said, "It's awesome—we've had heaps of work on lately". After all, busy is good—so speak of it in a positive way.

20 Get a Great Attitude—Do Not Worry if it is Out of your Control

Business Improvement

If you find yourself feeling or thinking negatively about something, then analyse it quickly. Spend five minutes and think about whether you fear something or examine the reasons behind your negativity. Then consider what you can do about it. For example, worrying about whether you will catch a cold from a sick co-worker will not achieve anything. If you know they have been sick, wipe down keyboards, phones etc with bacterial wipes and then move on—knowing you will NOT get sick. Some things are out of your control, so accept that and do not worry about it for any reasonable period of time.

21 Get a Great Attitude—Get Positive Friends

Business Improvement

Surround yourself with positive thinkers. If you have associates or friends who are always complaining or whinging, see less of them. If you have people who are positive, then make a point to see more of them.

22 Get a Great Attitude with Positive Affirmations

Business Improvement

Read positive affirmations daily. There are heaps of books out there with daily positive affirmations, or you can simply Google a site which sends you an email once a day. Have this as your little routine that you read one, once a day to have a positive start on your day. Or alternatively subscribe to a humour site and read one joke each morning to start your day.

23   Get a Great Attitude—Do Something Nice

Business Improvement

Do something nice. It is amazing how doing 'a good deed' for someone else, gives you that positive feeling. It might be that you donate some time to charity, or help someone else out or even just do something nice for someone, just for the sake of it. Remember the concept that 'what goes around, comes around' and of course 'you reap what you sow'.

24   Get a Great Attitude—Read a Book

Business Improvement

Read positive books. Select books which not only educate, but also motivate you. There are biographies about high flyers, sales and motivational books, success story books—so many to choose from, so have a read. If you are short on time, there are also many CD's available which you can listen to whilst driving in the car.

25   Get a Great Attitude—Get a Great Mentor

Business Improvement

Enlist the assistance of a mentor or coach or positive friend. If you know you have issues about being positive, or about your skills or abilities, often having a business coach or a mentor or (responsible and positive) friend can be of great assistance. Talking to that person about your personal challenges and your desire to change your attitude to one that is positive and productive is a good step in the right direction. Be sure that person has a mature, nurturing and positive attitude themselves—so that the 'right stuff' rubs off on you.

26 Get a Great Attitude—Have Faith

Believe in yourself. Do not allow yourself to say "I can't do that" or that "my business will never reach that level". Instead, think about what you might achieve and then think further about how you will achieve that goal.

Successful businesses do not happen over night, but they do happen—a lot of hard work is required, plus of course, the right attitude. ☺

27 Get an Education

Knowledge is very important. One of the main reasons that a business fails is due to the owners' lack of business knowledge. Maybe you do not understand how debtors affect your cash flow, or how best to use your marketing dollars, or what is the best way to network. Possibly you do not have a financial background, or you do not know the in's and out's of employing staff. However, if you are running a small business, you will not have a boardroom full of experts on the payroll.

Many things you will have to learn yourself. Reading books, listening to the advice of professionals or researching topics of need will increase your business knowledge.

However, do remember, you do not have to do it all yourself as your "team" may include part-time members. Remember that your accountant can be a valuable member of your team, or your solicitor. But they are not mind readers—if you have a question, or don't understand something, ask! I cannot re-iterate that enough.

Asking questions is not the signifier of stupidity or being dumb. In fact, quite the opposite. If you don't have a degree in accounting, or law, then of course you do not know every aspect of these professionals, so there is no such thing as a "dumb question". Pick their brains, take notes and learn. Your business will be better for it.

28 Get a Mentor or Business Coach

Business Improvement

Some business owners or operators think only failing businesses need a business coach. This is wrong. If your business has room for improvement or an increase in success—then there is room for a business coach. A business coach works for anyone who is dedicated to their business. So honestly, if you are not going to follow their advice, do their homework or action their guidance, then business coaching is a waste of money. BUT, do the work, follow the plan, action the homework and I can assure you, you will see results. The business coach will pay for him/herself ten-fold. The benefits of a business coach include:

- Improved sales and profit from having someone knowledgeable show you how
- They will help you with your team/staff—valuable pointers and guidance
- They will help you re-discover your passion, give you back that motivation and drive
- They will help you find clarity—what's important to you
- They will help you define your goals and aims
- They will help you focus—how to achieve those goals—the actual steps you need to take
- They will link you to information or sources of other information. If you need a great accountant, I'll bet they know one and will refer you

- They will help you navigate changes in the economy and market place.
- They will speed up the process of success. They are experts, they know what works and doesn't and know the strategies to test, measure and record. Don't waste time on activities which don't work.
- They will be someone impartial to whom you can complain, vent and express. Then of course they will re-direct you back on track to resolve your frustrations.
- They will provide a second opinion. Often, especially as small business owners, we have no-one we can ask for an opinion. Asking staff or clients may be unsuitable, or perhaps you don't have family at home who understand what you do, or maybe they are just sick of hearing about business all the time. Have an expert you can run ideas past.
- The best of all, they will be someone you are accountable to. Are your staff going to say to you, "Hey Donna, you haven't put xyz strategy in place yet!" You are accountable to your business coach . . . . They will demand results, push you, prod you and yes, when you achieve, congratulate you.
- Who will be unbiased. They are not personally involved, they are unbiased and separate from your business. They don't have a vested interest; e.g. as compared to a spouse who wants to see more of you, or a client who would love a rate decrease . . . they will be honest AND they are far enough out of the business that they can "see the forest through the trees".

And yes, I have used a business coach. Nathan McDonald of Black Belt Business helped me achieve results in so many ways. A big thank you!

Whether you are 40, 60 or 80, you should be always considering your exit strategy when you are operating your business. Your options may be to:

- Sell the business
- Wind it down and close it
- Sell/give to employees via employee purchase plans
- Leave to your offspring or relatives
- Remain indefinitely, but reduce your input and participation

Now, let's look at selling your business. You need to set up and have in place processes and procedures that mean the business will operate without you there. In order to sell your business (without moving house) your business cannot operate out of your home. You will also need to build up the business so that the figures are very healthy, in order to get the best possible price.

If you are planning to step back, how well do you know yourself? Do you know you can "let go" and take a back step? Are you the type of person who has to be involved and have a say on everything? You may have some learning of yourself to do and to develop the discipline to release control of day-to-day activities.

Likewise, if you are planning on leaving it to your children, then be sure this is what **they** want. Not every person is going to want to follow in Mummy or Daddy's footsteps and they may in fact have other aspirations or dreams. Be realistic, is your offspring suitable to run the business; do they have the nous, dedication and skills to fill your shoes? Look at this objectively and not passionately. Maybe it is **your** dream that your son/daughter takes over the family business but is this realistic? If they are keen, it may be they need training, which might take some time. It may be too, that you need a "Plan B" in place. What happens to your plan to have your son or daughter take over the business if his/her partner is transferred overseas? Be the proverbial boy scout and "be prepared".

30 Why do Businesses Lose Customers?

Business Improvement

Have a look at how we lose customers (or clients) and then you will know what you need to do to retain your customers (or clients). Here are the statistics on why the average business loses its customers:

68% of customers stop dealing with businesses because the staff give indifferent service and show little interest in them or their problems (this may be a perceived indifference)

9% of customers believe they can buy more cheaply elsewhere

8% of customers, one can never satisfy

7% of customers change firms on the recommendation of friends

4% of customers float from one business to another

3% of customers move away

1% die

Wow!! This says so much and yet, be honest—how often are you or your staff indifferent with your clients or customers? Do you build relationships with them and make them feel like they are special? Do you value their business and communicate this to them? Do you give them the opportunity to give you feedback (and welcome that feedback), especially if they are not happy? Just concentrate on that 68% and I believe the 9% of those who would otherwise buy more cheaply elsewhere may actually think twice if they are happy with your business. The 7% of those who move as a result of friends' recommendations, I believe would be far less inclined to do so if they were totally happy.

That's a huge chunk of business you can keep by not allowing you (or your staff) to be indifferent.

Remember, if someone is unhappy they will tell on average 10 people . . . but if they are happy, only about one person, so this means we really do have to work hard to build (and keep) good reputations and happy customers. Be sure you and your staff have the right mindset.

Etiquette in Business

"Good manners are essential for civilised living. They make life more enjoyable and less stressful, and they give pleasure".

—*Ita Buttrose*

INTRODUCTION TO ETTIQUETTE IN BUSINESS

Okay, now I know for a lot of you this is just plain, common sense good manners. Why would I possibly think tips on etiquette are suitable to include in a business improvement book? Well, in all my years of business, networking, business functions, dinners, lunches etc, I have experienced these occurrences on a regular basis, so I think this needs to be said.

31 Table Manners—Do not Eat & Talk at Once

Etiquette

Yes, I know it is a business meal, and yes, you will be talking, but do not do both at once. It is in very poor form and you are most likely going to end up spraying your co-diner with food out of your mouth. Take small bites and if a question is asked just as you have taken a bite, then make eye contact with the person, nod (indicating you have heard) and finish chewing and swallowing before you reply. Needless to say, do not chew with your mouth open. Do not slurp your coffee or soup.

32 Table Manners—Do not use a Mobile Phone

Etiquette

It is amazing how many people just whip out the old mobile phone at the dinner table. This is such bad form and it is extremely rude to the people you are dining with, regardless of whether it is a five star restaurant, café, coffee shop or even McDonalds.

If you are dining alone there is still no excuse as you are interrupting other diners, as most often, mobile phone users tend to speak louder.

And following on from this, if you are in a business meeting, turn off your mobile, or at least switch it to silent. If there is a critical call you have to take, explain this, and take that call ONLY. I have been in numerous business meetings, where the other person just continues to answer their phone during our meeting. If you do this, you send three clear messages to the person you are with:

1. You do not value their time or consider their time important.
2. You don't know how to organise yourself and are a reactive person, not proactive.
3. You have no manners.

Seriously, is that the message you want to send to prospective business associates, clients or colleagues? Do not believe you impress anyone by looking busy or popular. It is not only unprofessional, it is rude.

33 Table Manners—Cutlery is There to Use

Etiquette

You may not know which knife to use for which course, but simple manners apply. Use cutlery, use your napkin (it's meant to go in your lap before you commence eating) and do not throw your cutlery around or clang it loudly, such as when mixing sugar in your coffee. Think about what you are ordering too; I love spaghetti, but it is terribly messy and I never order it when dining out.

34 Table Manners—Put your Cutlery Together When you have Finished

Etiquette

I think a lot of people forget this one. When you are "at rest" during your meal, you can leave your knife and fork apart, sitting on your plate. Once you finish you should put your knife and fork neatly together in the middle of the plate. This signifies to a reasonably well trained waiter, that you are finished and they can remove your plate.

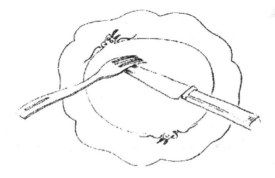

The correct positioning of a knife and fork when resting during a meal.

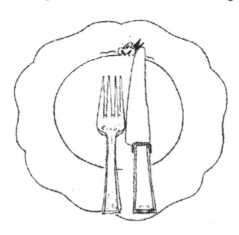

The correct positioning of a knife and fork when finished a meal.

35

Table Manners—Who Pays?

Etiquette

Regardless of gender, if it is a business function, generally it is quite acceptable for you each to pay for your own meal or coffee. One person (particularly the person who initiated the invitation) may say they will pick up the bill. Accept this graciously, be sure to say thank you and comment that "the next one will be on me". And, be sure to reciprocate. I used to actually write in my diary against the lunch who paid, so when the next one came up, I knew, before the bill even came, if it was my turn to pay. But regardless of what happens, do not make a big deal of it and of course, if it is their turn to pay, do not order the most expensive item on the menu. If the other person pays, don't forget some good, old-fashioned manners and say thanks.

36

Table Manners—Do not Overdo the Booze

Etiquette

Quite often alcohol will be present at a business function and it might even be free. Feel free to have a drink (particularly at evening or cocktail functions), but do not go overboard and drink up. Really, one or two drinks are enough if it is a business function or you are entertaining clients or staff. Even at the staff Christmas party, where all the staff might get quite inebriated, it does not mean you need to as well. Certainly enjoy a couple with the staff, but do not be one of the most intoxicated.

37 Personal Hygiene—Bad Breath should be Avoided

I must say, whether it is a social situation, romantic situation or business situation, bad breath is a massive turn off. Here are some practical tips:

- Practice good dental hygiene to ensure your teeth and gums are healthy
- Brush at least morning and evening (and if you know you are prone to bad breath, consider keeping a brush and toothpaste in your bag, briefcase or drawer)
- Use products such as breath mints, Listerine Strips, liquid mouthwash etc
- Have mints in the office; if you need to sit next to someone, for example for some training, take a mint first.
- If you are a smoker; be sure to fully exhale several times after smoking before coming back inside as often the smoke remains in your lungs for several breaths.

38 Personal Hygiene—Use a Deodorant

You should use a deodorant every morning after your shower (or even if you have showered at night) and if you know you are prone to body odour, have a spare on you and reapply as necessary. If you work with someone who does regularly smell, take them aside (or wait until you are alone) and briefly mention they need to reapply their deodorant. I know they may feel a little uncomfortable (as might you) but you are doing them a favour. I believe it is far better to discreetly mention the issue up front, than for the person to get a reputation or nickname such as "stinky".

39

Personal Hygiene—Do not Sneeze and Cough

You should cover your mouth if you sneeze or cough and then wash your hands—especially if you are going to shake hands. And, I suggest you wash your hands after shaking hands if possible (but of course extremely discreetly) as many germs are passed on through physical contact. It is also wise to have antiseptic wipes in the office and if you are a little ill, wipe down phones, mice, keyboards etc before someone else uses them. If you are open about the hygiene when you are ill, others will follow your lead. After all, you don't want to share the germs and have half the staff away sick.

Goals, Plans & Objectives

"Businesses don't plan to fail—they fail to plan!"—Well known business phrase.

"A good plan is like a road map; it shows the final destination and the best way to get there".

—H Stanley Judd (Writer).

INTRODUCTION TO GOALS, PLANNING & OBJECTIVES

For me this is a critical part of any business, and as a bookkeeper by trade, I am totally in my comfort zone with plans, lists, checklists—all neatly typed and well thought out. For you, maybe a scrap book, or exercise book will work just as well. The tip is to write it down in some way and give **thought** to your goals and objectives. Where do you want to be? How will you get there?

40 Set your Goals

Goals, Plans & Objectives

A pretty simple statement and no doubt those of us who have been around awhile have heard this many times? Yet, how many of us really plan properly?

Do you plan your day?
Do you plan your week?
Do you plan the next 90 days?
Have you written down your goals for the year?
Have you written down your goals for your life?

So if I asked you the question "where do you want to be in ten years time", do you know? Maybe you have a certain desire which isn't specific? It may be something like:

"I want to have a great business"
"I want to be a rich"
"I want to be successful".

Great, but these goals are not specific and are vague at best. How do you determine what a successful business is? What is rich? I bet I could ask 20 people to put a dollar value to the term "rich" and I would get close to 20 different answers.

So here is what I suggest—write up a goal sheet. Break it up into time zones:

- Goals to be achieved within 12 months
- Goals to be achieved within 5 years
- Goals to be achieved by retirement
- Goals to be achieved before death.

This does not have to be just about business. Certain goals may be linked, for example, you may want to include your goal to achieve $x sales AND to work a 20 hour week. Your goal sheet may also have categories, such as:

- Self
- Family
- Work
- Home
- Relationships
- Finances
- Community
- Knowledge
- Spirituality

Maybe you want to include starting a hobby you have always wanted to do, or perhaps it might be writing a book (one of my own!) or to get onto a Board, become better at golf or to complete a Masters degree.

Determine your goals and then determine which time zone they fit into. Now the important thing here is to **write it down!** I cannot stress that enough. Thinking is good, but putting those thoughts onto paper is the first step to achieving those goals.

41 Attach Activities to how you will Achieve your Goals

So you have set your goals. Now is the hard part. How will you achieve those goals? Maybe one of your goals was to save for a deposit on a house? Perhaps the activity to work towards that goal is to put $100 a week aside in a savings account; or better yet, set up an automatic sweep to that savings account. There may be three or four strategies or activities for each of those goals.

So, do you see where I am coming from here? You set your goals and then *plan* how you will achieve those goals. Think of this like travelling to a destination. You determine where you want to go, and then plan how you will get there. Take this street; turn right at that road, etc.

My Goals—as of April 2011

Goal	Action Required to Reach that Goal
Save Deposit for a House within 2 years	• Auto transfer $150 per week to savings • Set up personal budget • Sacrifice shoes—one pair per half year • Work two hours overtime/wk • Cut takeaway to once a week • After 6 months, increase savings to $200

So now you have a one page Goal Sheet, set up as a table (refer to table on prior page), where the left side is your goal and right side is how you will achieve that goal:

Then finally, type up the plan, laminate it and stick it somewhere you will see it every day. That might be inside your shower, or on the back of the toilet door, or in the front of your diary. Place your plan somewhere you will look at it regularly.

42 Do a Business Plan

Goals, Plans & Objectives

A business plan is a document in which you plan how you will operate your business. It will include how you market, a SWOT analysis, staff, marketing, policies, branding etc. I know there are companies out there that sell business plans or do them for you but I strongly suggest you do your own, and the reason is that part of the process of planning goes towards improving your business. A business plan does not have to be a 50 page formal document; you can keep it far shorter and simpler. Reviewing your plan helps you review your business.

You can get a template on how to do a business plan off the internet or from a business coach. Once you do it, it is a good idea to review it regularly. Some suggest reviewing your plan every three months, personally I find once a year is enough.

43 Do a SWOT Analysis

As part of a traditional business plan, often a SWOT analysis is done. SWOT stands for strengths, weaknesses, opportunities and threats. However, you do not have to do this with a business plan; instead you may choose to do it separately. Rather than doing this in your head, take a moment, grab a note book and write this down. AND if you did a SWOT analysis a few years back, maybe it is time for a re-visit, as let's face it, the business world is constantly changing.

Now here is a TIP: do this with a couple of your team/staff and you'll be surprised at the ideas that come up. Let's look at each area:

Strengths—This is pretty easy, it is essentially the strengths of your business. What makes you better than your competitors? Why do your clients or customers buy from you? It might be that you have a fantastic product, or because you are a home-based service and your prices are reasonable due to lower overheads. Maybe you have a great after sale service, or perhaps you train your team to be the best or possibly you have a niche market. Write down your strengths and do not forget them when you are writing marketing material or talking to prospective new customers or clients.

Weaknesses—Okay, this is harder and you do need to be honest. Where do your weaknesses lie? What could you work more on? But the great thing about a weakness is that there is heaps of room for improvement. So what are *your* business' weaknesses? Perhaps you have high staff turnover and therefore standards are not met, or maybe your product isn't consistently performing. Perhaps you do not have a heap of experience in your field, or you don't market your business well because your expertise lies in your industry/field, not in marketing.

Opportunities—Where do the opportunities lie for growth in your business? Would franchising be suitable? Could you form a strategic alliance with another great business, or group of businesses to grow? Could your product be a hit overseas and therefore be exported? Is there a need for your service in remote areas of your State? Write all these ideas down.

Threats—Whilst not a pleasant thought, they need to be reviewed. For example, in the Bookkeeping and Accounting profession, if the Government said businesses did not need to lodge a BAS or do a tax return, how would this affect the industry? Threats could be changes in legislation, changes in policy, power strikes, a competitor coming in with something bigger and better, fire, riots, changes in industrial relations rules or perhaps even your computer crashing.

Now, once you have reviewed each of these, you then need to plan on how to make the most (or reduce the affect) of each of the above. A SWOT analysis isn't just about identifying, but about finding solutions or strategies to improve and strengthen your business.

Strengths—now you see your strengths listed—think about how you can grow your business utilising these strengths.

Weaknesses—so what are you going to do to overcome these? If your product is not consistently performing well, then review the systems of production, quality assurance and get the product right, first time, every time.

Opportunities—now that these are identified, how are you going to make the most of these ideas? If you see a great opportunity, grab it with both hands and make the most of it. Of course research the idea fully and sensibly—but we all know the adage "nothing ventured, nothing gained". The great success stories in business are about people who identified opportunities and optimised that situation.

Threats—do not believe "it won't happen to me!" How many people who have met with disaster had that thought! It might be as simple as insurance, or possibly having a great offsite backup system. It might be diversifying your business. It might mean being flexible and keeping ahead of the trends or having ready an action plan in the eventuality of disaster.

Yes, I know, some of you are saying "but I don't have time to sit down and do all this review—I've got sales to make, and invoices to issue and staff to supervise . . .". Remember "businesses do not plan to fail—THEY FAIL TO PLAN!" Schedule some time now in your diary in the next week or two for planning and get that SWOT analysis done.

44 Do a Business 90 Day Plan

Goals, Plans & Objectives

Those who have worked with a business coach will be familiar with the concept of the 90 day plan. Simply put, it is a plan for the next three months. I have always done mine on an Excel spreadsheet. You simply write down some goals for the quarter. It might be that you want to increase your sales turnover by 15%. So you list this goal and then break the spreadsheet up into 13 weeks (90 days). Then you plan on how you will achieve this specific goal. Perhaps in week one you will do a Google Adwords campaign. Possibly in week three you will promote a special offer to your current clients. Let's say week five will see you running an advertisement in the local paper. Etcetera. Much like the Goals sheet above, you are writing down each goal for the quarter and the specific steps you will take to achieve that goal BUT you actually will determine WHEN you will take those steps.

Then of course at the beginning of each week you look at what you have to do. As you do the action, you mark it off (I yellow out the box in Excel to designate it's done) and then at the end of the week you review your list of tasks (or actions) for the week and ensure all have been done. This simple method ensures that you:

1. Set goals
2. Set activities to reach those goals
3. Action those activities.

Finally at the end of the quarter you look at your sales as compared to those of the previous quarter, to see if you have achieved your objective of a 15% increase. If I achieved my goal, I would give myself a little reward. So reward yourself, possibly a long weekend away with the family, or a particular bracelet you've been eyeing at the local shopping centre, or that new golf club you really want but can't really justify.

45   Daily or Weekly Plans

Goals, Plans & Objectives

You should also have a daily/weekly plan sheet. You might use an electronic organiser, MS Outlook Tasks or the simple but effective diary. Let's say you use a diary. Rule a line down the middle of the page. On the left side are your appointments, and on the right side are your tasks or things you have to do that day. As a new task comes to mind, write it down. It might be a tax bill to pay, or possibly something you have promised to send out to a prospective new client. Write it down.

At the beginning of your day, take five minutes to review your day's tasks and diary. See where you have to go and what you have to do. As you action each task put a line through it, or use a highlighter pen to mark it off. Then at the end of the day do another quick review and check that everything is done. It can be immensely satisfying to see a page with all your tasks highlighted—you did everything you were supposed to do that day. And, it means you did not forget anything important!

Personally I am a lists person. Whilst I have a great memory, I have so many trillion things to remember every day—not just for my business, but also for my family, my children, my staff—if I do not keep notes, lists and tasks, then little things are sure to slip through the cracks. If you miss a client meeting, or forget to make a phone call as promised, your reputation may be affected, or possibly a prospective new customer will not be impressed or you could receive a tax fine for a late payment. Being efficient, organised and using lists does help you both personally and in your business—so start simply and think about a system which will work for you and start using it—today!

With regard to all the above plans, I am not saying you have to do them all. Perhaps you simply want to do the SWOT analysis and then have 90 day plans. Personally, I get heaps more out of the 90 day plan than I do the whole business plan. However, having said that, often Banks and other financial institutions perceive a business with a Business Plan in a better light . . . it all depends on what your needs are and what works for you.

Kids, Family & Home-Based Businesses

"Stay committed to your decisions, but stay flexible in your approach. It's the end you're after".

—Anthony Robbins (Motivational Speaker).

*Remember **why** you wanted to work from home!*

INTRODUCTION TO KIDS, FAMILY & HOME BASED BUSINESS

Working from home definitely has advantages; ranging from zero travel time, to being there with family and saving the overhead cost of rent. And there is the further appeal of no office politics, greater flexibility and added independence. But to work happily from home does take some effort.

46 Working from Home— Setting up the Environment

Kids, Family & Business

Working from home can be a great thing, but it takes balance and discipline and of course you need to set up yourself professionally. Your office space needs to be well thought out. Working from the kitchen table is not a good idea as you are disjointed, will have to pack up every night and you are not in a work frame of mind when you sit at the dining table. Of course, if clients are likely to visit your premises you will need to have a professional environment. Whether it is a garage or a converted bedroom, it should look like an office, not like the garage, or worse, a dungeon. You should consider making the environment one which is functional for you and one in which you are likely to be productive. It should be a place in which you want to spend time. If you feel cluttered or disorganised or if the space is dreary, are you really going to want to be there? Ensure you can access files easily, that it is neat, you have your equipment set up well, and it is well lit and an environment that makes you feel positive. Some of these things will cost money, such as efficient computer equipment, but other things, such as a fresh coat of paint, a nice print on the wall, or a lovely green plant, don't need to cost a fortune. Remember this is about your business, so not only are these expenses often tax deductible, but also you have to spend money to make it.

47 Working from Home—Have the right Equipment

Have the right equipment. Just as your office space needs to be functional, so does your equipment. Ensure you have excellent broadband, a fast computer and whatever else equipment is relevant to your business. You have saved money on rent so do not be stingy on the tools which will help you earn your living.

48 Working from Home—Workplace Health & Safety (WH&S)

Be Workplace Health &Safety conscious. Just like any work environment, you need to be conscious of having a safe working environment—especially if you employ staff. Is lighting sufficient, do you have quality ergonomic chairs, is your desk at the right height? This is a business, so be sure to cover WH&S issues as well, including an emergency evacuation procedure.

49 Working from Home—Obey Local Council

Kids, Family & Business

Regarding rules and regulations—firstly be sure to find out what local council requirements are relevant for your area including those related to the specific zoning of the land on which your home stands. Many Councils impose restrictions on activities, particularly those which generate noise, have heaps of visitors, or perhaps they may restrict the number of staff you may have working on the premises. Research whether you are required to pay a fee or gain a licence in order to operate your business.

50 Working from Home—Suitable Storage Space

Kids, Family & Business

Have suitable storage space. As the ATO requires us to keep business records for five years, be aware of how much space these records can consume. You might find that the cupboard in the corner just won't cope. Have sufficient space, or source somewhere else to store these records—a location which is clean, dry, free of vermin and readily accessible in case you do need to access any of these records.

51 Working from Home—Make it Deductible

Kids, Family & Business

Ideally have a separate access area. This will have an impact on what you can claim as household business deductions but also means your business and home areas are separate. The kitchen table is not a place to conduct business.

52

Working from Home—Avoid (legally) Capital Gains Tax

Kids, Family & Business

Capital Gains Tax. Be sure to speak to your accountant about what you can claim as a business deduction. Generally, if you claim a percentage of your house building insurance, rates, and mortgage repayments, then these will trigger a possible capital gains tax debt. Remember your home, if it's your principle place of residence, would not normally be subject to Capital Gains Tax when you sell—so don't set yourself up to the possibility of having to pay this additional tax because you claimed a few deductions.

53

Make your Family Important Too!

Kids, Family & Business

If you have been a business owner and a parent at the same time, then you know it is damn hard work to do it all and do it all successfully. Some days you just wish you did not need to sleep so you could fit in everything.

As you look at business and plan your day and what you do, so too you need to plan your family and specifically your family time. I started my business ten years ago when my three children were only three, seven and ten. I did not have to deal with changing a nappy whilst on the phone to an important client, but I did have my kids saying things like "You love your computer more than us" or "You love your clients more than me". The fact is that I didn't, but I was very determined to make the business successful and still be a good mum.

I am not a child psychologist, or a paediatrician or child expert, I'm just a mum who has been through it all and I think I (and my kids) came out the other end pretty much intact. So, here is my first point.

Prioritise—there are times when the business is the most important thing. I would not miss a client deadline so that I could do tuckshop duties or pick up my kids' toys. I determined what was important and each person's need would vary according to the importance. I did miss a string of client appointments one day when my oldest broke his arm and I had to go to hospital with him. At that point in time he was the most important thing. At other times, I've had to decline kicking the soccer ball around as I had some client BASes to lodge. At that point in time the clients' lodgements took priority. And yes, that is the time when my kids thought I loved the computer, my clients or my staff more. They did tend to forget I have always been there when it counted. But do not let kids do the guilt trip on you—you know in your own heart if you are a good mum or dad. And if you think you are lacking, then it is up to you to do something about it. Go back to your time schedule and decide if you can cut some work hours to spend time with the kids.

54   Set aside Family Time

Kids, Family & Business

When I started out in business I used to work weekends and nights. I absolutely almost never do now. I do not go to evening business networking functions, I rarely make client appointments at night and I don't work on the computer after dinner. You may have to do this when you start out, but set a deadline for this and communicate that time span with your family. Maybe it is twelve months and then you will cut back. Ensure you keep your promise and do cut back. Now, I just say that I do not work evenings as this is my "family time" and guess what? Most people accept (and respect) this. I start work about 4:30am. So by 4pm in the afternoon my work day is done. I then switch to family mode—homework, chauffeuring to sport, making dinner, doing the washing etc. This is my family and 'me' time.

Another tip is to diarise personal time. For example, I play netball on a Wednesday morning. I have done so for years. It is my special 'me' time. It is written in my diary every Wednesday morning so that neither I nor my staff book an appointment during that time. However, one tip, I now write "NB" in my diary and say it is a standard booking, as I have had clients look over my shoulder and say that I can cancel netball and book them in as their business is more important. And yes, whilst their business is more important than my sport, you have to be firm and stick to your guns. You can do the same for your family. Diarise if you are going to train the kids' footy team on a Tuesday afternoon, or if you want to help with class reading at your child's school on a Thursday morning. Diarise it and stick to it.

55 Be Efficient with your Time

Kids, Family & Business

Be time efficient on all fronts, if you can save some time, now that is more time you can spend with your partner or children. For example, I never go to an appointment without something to do; especially places like the doctor or dentist where you could be waiting 5 minutes to 50 minutes. Reading is ideal; business magazines, newsletters, reports, or material you have to check.

Another idea is to multitask—but not two important tasks at once; you will not do either well, but if you are on the phone to someone, clean your desk at the same time. Putting pens in the drawer requires no brainpower, but doing it later takes time. Another possibility is to do something else whilst you are driving. Either return phone calls (not those you would need to take notes—and of course only using hands free) or listen to the kids' spelling in the morning whilst driving them to school.

Bulking up is another great time saver. When you cook something like Spaghetti Bolognese, do a double batch and freeze one; you will really appreciate that quick meal after a busy day and can avoid resorting to take-away for the twentieth time.

I have become a wonderful delegator, once I got past the belief that (as a perfectionist) no-one could do it as well as me. Delegating to a cleaner, or having a bookkeeper is time saving within the business but you can also involve your children in your business and for example use it as a way in which they can earn pocket money. An eight year old can easily manage (and even enjoy) shredding. A twelve year old (once shown) can do basic filing. It is not "slave labour" as your older children may chime; you are teaching them the valuable lesson of developing a work ethic, teaching them skills, preparing them to be able to write a great resume AND you are getting help AND spending time with them.

And don't forget the best lesson of all that you are teaching them—that money does not grow on trees—it has to be earned.

56 Structure your Day and Week

Kids, Family & Business

Structure your work day and week. In other words—develop a routine. Just because you are working at home, do not forget to have structure to your day. Plan your work week and day, what you will do and when. Maybe marketing day is Tuesday, or Wednesday morning is debt collections, or Thursday afternoon is working on your business plan etc. Set a structure, be realistic about it, and try to stick to it.

57

Have Regular Scheduled Breaks

Kids, Family & Business

Have regular breaks. As above, set a lunch hour, but it's also a good idea to set a short break for morning tea and afternoon tea. Often (especially if you work alone) you get engrossed in what you are doing, and before you know it, it's six hours later. Don't laugh, but maybe setting break times up in your phone as a reminder to stop is needed. You need to take regular breaks to look after yourself and to ensure you operate at maximum efficiency.

58

Track your Time

Kids, Family & Business

Track your time. Because we work from home, again losing track of time, we discover we are in fact working a 60 to 90 hour week. Track your time and set limits for yourself. There was a reason in the first place you wanted to work from home—don't lose that clarity.

59

Avoid Interruptions

Kids, Family & Business

Avoid interruptions. If a salesman catches you at home, you do not have to listen to his spiel for 20 minutes. Politely advise them you are working, and close the door. Ditto regarding telemarketers. Unless they have something you are interested in, chances are they are unnecessarily taking up your valuable time. Registering on the "Do not call" register might be wise too. And finally, close the door to your office.

60

Block Out External Noises

Kids, Family & Business

Block out external noises. If you do have family at home and someone else is caring for them (especially younger children), then closing the door might not be enough. Maybe using an iPod or music via headphones which blocks out the noise will do the trick.

61

Educate your Visitors

Kids, Family & Business

Gently educate friends, family and visitors. When you let your friends and family know you are working from home, try to send the message at the same time that it's best they "book" drop in time with you, or alternatively let them know that you are going to make Friday afternoons social time, as you are trying to operate a business and work to set hours. I know this can be difficult; you do not want to offend, but you cannot just have drop-ins all the time, or you will get nothing done.

However, some people don't get subtle hints; you might have to be a little firm, and although you are really glad to see them, you just can't stop at present as you are working on an important deadline, but could you catch up with them, perhaps Friday afternoon?

62

Set Clear Limits—Whilst Working and When

If you are a home-based business, then you know how hard it is to stay focussed on what you do whilst working and then the control it takes to not just keep working past the end of your work day, or just wander into the office to check if that email you are waiting for has arrived. You have to learn discipline. Firstly the discipline to keep on task and keep working and not get distracted by the fridge, TV or washing machine. Then of course you have to learn when to stop and walk away from the office.

When you have children (who are old enough to understand), explain to them that when you are in the office and working, they should try to not interrupt you. Define your work times, communicate them clearly with your family and <u>stick to your set times</u>! If the kids know you work until 4pm and then will come out and spend time with them, they will learn to wait; but be prepared, pens down at 4pm sharp! Keep your promises.

Even if you don't have children, I strongly suggest you run to set office hours, such as 8am to 4pm and stop for an hour for lunch. In your "lunch break" you can watch Oprah, or put on another load of washing, but not during your work hours. As you are working from home, you can work around your natural schedule, for example, start at 5am if you are a morning person, but ensure you finish early too.

My kids would often want me to take them somewhere or do something with them. Giving myself a realistic amount of time to finish the task I was working on, I would tell them that I would be done by say 4:15pm. They then knew that at 4:15 they could walk in and say "let's go Mum" and know that I would get up then and there and go. I will admit this was hard at first, as often I did not estimate the time accurately and they would return at 4:15 only for me to say "just another 5 minutes" which of course meant really another half hour. Be realistic with these times and stick to your word.

63 Teach your Kids about Business

It has amazed me at how some people have no idea about basic concepts within business. One new business owner needed me to teach him how to write a cheque. I had a junior staff member once who had no idea what "banking" was. The first thing I think you can do for your kids is involve them in your business. Explain what you do. I've had many a discussion in the car on the way to school about small business, bookkeeping, work practices etc. Of course you have to edit the discussion according to the age of your child. For example, I have talked about franchises and why someone would get into a franchise with my then 14 year old. Remember many business skills can benefit anyone in life; whether it is how to use a computer, write a cheque or do the banking.

When you get your children to help you with tasks within your business you are teaching them life skills. Kids are sponges and they learn things very quickly. Hand them money without them having to earn it and they sure will get used to it quickly; when it comes to working for someone, they will have no (good) work ethic. I have had office juniors in my own business who initially thought it was fine to sit and chat, use their mobile, send text messages or sit doing nothing. Short of winning Gold Lotto, I have not yet come across a way where people just give you money for nothing—I have to work hard for it and so do my children.

My now 20 year old was shocked years ago when he did not get the full $10 for mowing the front lawn; I gave him only $7. He stood there and wanted to know why I had "short changed" him. He had done a shocking job; he had missed an entire area and so I said that I wasn't satisfied and would not be paying in full. If a client of mine was not satisfied with the job I had done, they would not pay me in full; I would have to either rectify the problem or accept only part payment—if I was lucky. Since that day, my son has mowed the lawn properly—and been paid—in full. Sometimes he even gets me to come out and "inspect" his work before putting away the mower.

64 Set Limits for Yourself

Kids, Family & Business

Set limits for yourself. Email is a notorious interrupter. Maybe you are on your way to bed, decide to just quickly scan your emails and two hours later you are still at it. Or you are in the kitchen making dinner and hear that "ding" of an incoming email and the next thing you know, the dinner is burning. Even though you live at work, don't "live at work". Turn off the computer, the sound or the monitor, if email "sucks you in".

65 Delegate (see Time Management section for more info on this)

Kids, Family & Business

Delegate. Being home based does not mean you have to do the office cleaning, or process the payroll or do the bookkeeping yourself. Do what you do well and outsource the rest. You might even consider a part-time assistant, office person or contractor for simple tasks.

66 Dress to Work

Dress to go to work. I know some people say it's great to work in their pyjamas, but for me, I really find I switch to business/work mode once I get dressed and go to work.

And of course, if you do have an unexpected drop in (business orientated) then you will not get caught out looking sloppy, unshaven or unprofessional.

67 Be Professional

Be professional. Just because you are working from home, it does not need to mean you are any less professional. Ensure your office space looks professional, that you have the latest equipment and answer the phone in a professional manner. If children are going to answer the phone, be sure to educate them to do this professionally, or don't allow it to happen, alternatively have separate phone lines for home and business. Again, home based does not need to equate to slack or casual. Have professional business cards, stationery, quotations, website etc.

68 Set Office Rules

Kids, Family & Business

Set office-related rules for your family too. Just like you should be professional in the office, set rules for your family. My kids were not allowed in the office during work hours, and definitely NOT when I had a client visiting. If they did come in, they could not be noisy, nor could they play in there and when they got older, they had to wear a shirt in there (as opposed to the "tanned Adonis" look).

69 Consider Meeting Alternatives

Kids, Family & Business

Use alternatives for meetings if your space is not as professional as you need. Whilst your home office may be okay for some clients, you may want to impress a new contact and not let on that you are home based. That's okay, offer to meet them at a local coffee shop, but check out those options first. Ensure your choice is easy to find, has good coffee, good service and looks a little upmarket. Also be aware of times of day; you may want to avoid the after school noise of parents with boisterous children.

70 Avoid Isolation

Kids, Family & Business

Avoid the isolation. Often working from home means you are alone. Now whilst this is a plus at some times (you can achieve a lot working alone) it can also give you a feeling of isolation. One tactic is to have music playing, but also you might like to schedule time into your day to meet people. Those people may be friends, networking contacts, or clients. In other words, have "people time" and keep up with both your personal and professional contacts.

71 Reward Yourself

Kids, Family & Business

If you are working alone, then you won't have someone there to motivate you, so you will need to motivate yourself. Set yourself some goals, and when you achieve those goals, have a reward in place, which will give you pleasure.

72 Consider a Coach

Kids, Family & Business

If you want your business to grow, then having a coach to support, guide and prompt you along the journey might just be the ticket. If your mentor was traditionally your boss at work, then you may need a business coach to fill this role and help your business grow.

73 Be Thankful

Kids, Family & Business

Finally, be thankful. Perhaps you have a boss who allows you to work from home, or a client who is happy with the arrangement; be sure to thank them and appreciate all the benefits of working from home.

Networking

"The most important single ingredient in the formula of success is knowing how to get along with people".

—*Theodore Roosevelt (26th US President).*

INTRODUCTION TO NETWORKING

I actually chose to move networking out of the sales/ marketing chapter of this book. The reason being is that too often people think networking is only about selling. They could not be further from the truth. Put simply, networking is about building and developing relationships. Networking is about developing trust. Networking is NOT about closing the sale. If you are a very impatient person, I suspect you will find networking a challenge, as I believe this is something which requires time, patience and good people skills. However, networking is a very powerful business growth tool; done well it will make a huge difference to your business and bottom line.

74

Networking is not about 'Closing the Deal'

Networking

Too often people think that networking is about making a sale *today*. Networking is about building relationships, which is something we all know, takes time. In marketing, it's said that someone needs to be exposed to something (such as an advert or flyer) at least four times to have the best affect. A similar concept occurs with networking; people need to get to know you, see you regularly and build up that rapport and trust that's necessary. Also please remember that it is very foolish to dismiss the person you are speaking with because you figure they won't need your services. For example, if you run an elite babysitting business and you discover the person in front of you does not have children. Don't just wind it up and bolt. Perhaps that person has lots of friends or siblings with childcare issues.

75 Networking is not about Collecting as Many

Networking is about forming relationships. Just as some people think it's about closing the sale, or a quick deal, others think that the more business cards they collect the better. Now if your objective is not to network but actually to increase your database, then that's fine. But if you want to actually network, then actually don't aim at getting more than about three or four cards for a two-hour function. When you meet someone, talk to them. Maintain eye contact—do not be scanning the room for your next conquest. Listen. Ask them questions. Ideally let them do 70% of the talking and start to build that relationship. You will find by listening and asking questions, you will learn a great deal about that person, which down the track **may** help you do business with them. At some point during your discussion, get their business card. The next tip will tell you what to do with that card. Be genuine and friendly; do not be pressured to try and push your products or services at this time. Another tip is to keep moving; so after about 20 minutes, really nicely excuse yourself and move onto someone else. After all, you are there to network, so speaking to only one person for two hours takes you to the other extreme.

76 What to do with those Business cards after the Networking Function

Firstly, a great tip is to write on the card, where you met the person and a couple of words about them. For example, "Met Sunrise Breakfast 25.9.09—needs a bkr". Another tip is to use a white out strip if the card is one of those glossy ones you cannot write on directly. Always have a pen with you, as often at networking functions, you sit down for a meal or listen to a guest speaker—which can be a perfect moment to jot a few quick notes on business cards you've been given. Labelling your cards (or making quick notes) can be a smart idea—unless you have a photographic memory—which unfortunately, I don't.

Then, when you get back to the office, add them to your database, or email address book or whatever system you have to keep and track your contacts. If you think that person may be a good lead for you, then email them within a couple of days, saying it was nice to meet them and ask them if they would like to get a coffee and catch up? At this time, if their business card doesn't indicate, ask them what suburb they are based in. Good networkers will jump at the opportunity to meet again.

77 Arranging the Follow-up Meeting after the Networking Function

Networking

So, you have met someone, got their card and suggested meeting for a coffee and chat. When they accept, if they haven't already, suggest a coffee shop (Coffee Clubs in Brisbane are often excellent options; easy to find; flexible/full menus and somewhat prolific) geographically halfway between them and you. Provide three dates/times which suit you and ask if any of these would suit them. It is a good idea (to be time savvy) to arrange appointments within the vicinity of each other. And if you are really lucky, you might even be able to make the next one at the same place. I allow an hour for this meeting, but if you have another person coming; don't book them exactly one hour later. If the first meeting starts late, or overruns time, it is really awkward to boot out the first person whilst the second one hovers around.

Remember, you can take something to do between meetings if everyone is on schedule. When you agree on a time and place, write it all in your diary or enter into your PDA straight away and also jot down their mobile number. If you are going to be more than five minutes late, ring them and let them know; there is nothing worse than wondering if you are in the right place or if you have been "stood up".

78 What to do at the Follow-up Meeting after the Networking Function

Networking

Okay, this meeting you are getting down to business. Of course, start with the usual pleasantries; even try to draw the person out to talk about their family, pets or hobbies. Then ask them about their business and be attentive. When they have finished (and if they are experienced, they will actually ask you to discuss your business) then start telling them about your business. If you have let them go first, you have the advantage, because you have an idea of what they might need or how you can help them. Bring flyers, cards, brochures etc, but please, do not do the three-hour business spiel, working from flip cards etc. This is sure to turn off your guest. Be genuine, informative, but not too formal. Remember, it is a casual coffee, not a boardroom presentation. Also remember, it is not "all about me". If when talking to the person, you can help them out, jot down notes in a note pad (have a small one always handy). It might be they are looking for a good accountant, and you know some, and promise a referral. Or maybe you told them about a great local Chamber mentoring program and they are keen to know more. Jot this down. And absolutely, be sure to follow up on your promises and do what you promised.

79 Building Strategic Alliances can be a Business Maker

A strategic alliance is where one business (or person) works for or refers work to another similar or related business which is not a competitor. Often they are in related industries or sectors. An example is that a bookkeeping business might have alliances with an accounting firm. Many times clients say to their bookkeeper? "Do you know a good accountant" or to their accountant "do you know a good bookkeeper?" These two businesses can refer work back and forth and work together, very successfully.

Another example might be a bridal cake maker and florist. They could even promote each other, by having posters, business cards or 'special offer' flyers in each other's store. These businesses complement each other and can also refer work back and forth . . . it is a win-win situation. So when you meet someone, is this a situation where you can form a mutually beneficial alliance? Be sure you know about the other business and ideally know they provide as good a service/product as you do. A referral should be genuine where you believe your client or customer will really benefit from this other business. But remember, it is not all take and no give. It is always good to start the ball rolling and refer a friend, associate or client to that other business . . . hopefully they will reciprocate soon. But be patient, a quality referral may not occur overnight.

People & Communication

"People will not bear it when advice is violently given, even if it is well founded. Hearts are like flowers; they remain open to the softly falling dew, but shut up in the violent downpour of rain"

—*John Paul Richter.*

INTRODUCTION TO PEOPLE & COMMUNICATION

In almost every business we have, there is always an element of dealing with people. Yes, we may be technicians at times and have businesses that are not service orientated, or in the areas of hospitality or tourism, however, I cannot think of a business where you never deal with people. We deal with our customers, our suppliers, staff, associates and we need to communicate wisely and well in order to make those dealings effective.

80 Choose your Battles Wisely—You do not Always have to Win

If you have teenagers, you probably know exactly what I am talking about here. If every little thing was not done exactly as it was supposed to be, then you would spend your entire day chasing, rectifying or arguing. Is the issue worth having a fight with a staff member over? Perhaps one of your team arrived at work five minutes late—if it is not a repeated occurrence, then possibly it is wiser to not start a discussion which may blow into something far worse than the original offence. If you are talking with a customer, remember the adage "the customer is always right" . . . If they complain about something which you believe is unreasonable, then do not stand up and argue with them, or I can guarantee that customer will be a customer of yours no more. Diplomacy will help you out—and although you know you are right, just saying something like "I'm sorry you were not happy with the service we provided you—I'll talk to my staff about this" may help resolve the situation.

Some (but not all) customers complain just to try and get something free from businesses—so gauge the person. If they are a consistent complainer, and you have objectively listened and assessed the situation, then don't give them a freebie, but if you believe their complaint is just, then rectify it in some way. Often, just getting an apology or small credit, or sorry gift, is all that person wanted. They feel they have received due consideration and reached a favourable outcome, and more importantly, will use your services or product again as you have sent the message that you value their custom.

81 Sexual Harassment

People & Communication

We are in a time and place where we have to be very, very careful. An innocent action can be taken the wrong way and then you will find yourself in trouble. It is as simple as this—sexual harassment is illegal.

- Have a clear sexual harassment policy: so it is clear to all that sexual harassment is not acceptable and IF an employee has a concern, they know how they can raise that issue. Be clear that their complaint will be treated seriously and with confidentiality and ensure you do so. Addressing the issue internally may be far more beneficial than allowing it to go the next step.
- Do not touch your staff. A fathering hand on a young employee's shoulder can be taken the wrong way; maybe you are not even aware you are doing it, but the employee may be very uncomfortable—leading either to quitting or suing. Even a hand on the back of a female employee, leading into an elevator for example, which used to be considered "gentlemanly", can now be taken the wrong way. And do not do what a client of mine did—put your

hand on the employee's hand which was still on the computer mouse. I know he did it just because he wanted to move the mouse and is an impatient sort of person, but I could have taken it the wrong way and thought that he was "grabbing at me".

- Do not allow yourself (as a male) to be the last person in the workplace at the end of the day with a female employee. Have a policy that no less than three people are left at the end of the day, and have your staff leave together, not leaving you alone with staff. You may not do anything, but in an era of legal action, if the employee has a gripe with you, do not leave yourself "open". This tip is the same for sporting coaches if you have girls you coach . . . avoid being alone with them and never touch them, even if it is just to demonstrate a better position.
- Do not have sexually explicit pictures, photos, calendars, and screensavers in the workplace.
- Do not distribute sexually explicit emails to your staff, and ensure others do not. This should be part of your Sexual Harassment policy.
- Do not have an affair in the workplace, especially with a subordinate or employee. Even if you are single, and so is the other person, it is still not a good idea. You open up a whole can of worms, ranging from other staff assuming favouritism, to what will happen when the relationship ends? And if you (or the employee) are married, and word gets out then some people you do business with (and even your staff) may not want to continue dealing with you. Some people take this very seriously and would see you as an immoral person. If you are immoral in your personal life, then they may assume this follows on in your business life.
- Remember that sexual harassment is not always a male "perpetrator" with a female "victim". Ladies, we also need to watch our behaviour as much as the men, and of course sexual harassment can also be same sex, so don't think it's okay for say a lady to place her hand on another

female's leg. Remember, you may not mean anything by an action, but think about how it *might* be perceived by another person? Perception, rather than intent, can often be the key in these issues.

82 Understand Others' Motivations

People & Communication

In your dealings with people I believe it is good to understand others' motivations. Are they motivated by success, money, or a thirst for knowledge? Sometimes it is as simple as asking the other person what they would like to get out of, for example, a meeting? Sometimes it is good to know that your staff are not just motivated by money, they may well be seeking self improvement, job satisfaction or to have a happy day. Throwing money at them, when that is not a primary motivator, therefore will not achieve the best outcome. Do not assume your goals or motivators are the same as those of the next person. Ask the people you work with, and then consider if you can find a way to achieve their objectives. One example I had was that some of my team dearly wanted flexibility in their employment, because they had families—so providing the opportunity to work at home and offering flexible working arrangements was something important I could offer them as a fitting motivator.

83 Learn Personality Styles

People & Communication

There are a number of great personality type tests out there, including MBTI (Myer-Briggs Type Indicator) and DISC. You can gain training on one or more of these systems and I know there are books out there on both, as well as training workshops. The point here is that by knowing the personality type for a specific person, you can then talk their language. For example, with MBTI's if you know the person is a "T" (T being a person who bases their decisions on thoughts, rather than feelings) then if you are trying to convince them something, saying "it feels right" means little to them. Instead, giving them the facts of why it IS right will have a far better effect. On the DISC scene, if you know you are talking to a "D" (Director) then don't fluff around, don't go into long analysis. Just be succinct, give them the top points and don't waste their time. Regardless of your own personality style, if you talk the language of the personality style of the other person, then you will be talking their language.

Personal Development

"There are no shortcuts to any place worth going".

—*Beverly Sills (Opera Singer).*

INTRODUCTION TO PERSONAL DEVELOPMENT

And like the chapter quote, personal development is something which does not just happen overnight. Learning is something which I believe you never stop doing. I look back now over the last almost 30 years since I left school, and I think I have learnt more since leaving school than during school. (I'm not knocking school at all, but life is an amazing educator). We learn new things every day, if we have our minds open—and I for one plan to keep learning, to the day I draw my last breath.

84 Wisdom is worth its Weight in Gold—
We are Never too old to Learn

Personal Development

Whether you have a Uni degree or twenty years in the trade, there is always room for improvement. Regardless of what field you are in, you should always look at improving yourself. Do courses, improve your skills and seek advice at every opportunity. Often you learn heaps from asking questions or even researching information on the internet. Go to your local bookstore and look in the business section. And when you get the book (like this one) be sure to actually open it and read it. Having a wonderfully full bookshelf is of no benefit to you if you don't actually read the material. Set aside an hour a week to read. It might be a Saturday morning, or Friday afternoon, but make it a time you will stick to. Perhaps getting up ten minutes earlier every morning may work for you.

There is also a wealth of information and resources available online for small business, for example, the Queensland's Government's

"Small Business Solutions" have many services available as well as a great mentoring program. Other state (and federal) government websites also offer helpful resources for small businesses. Tap into these services and get ahead of the rest. Some great webpage links include:

Small Business Solutions
www.smallbusinesssolutions.qld.gov.au

Government Workshops
www.business.qld.gov.au/workshops

Business Performance Checks
www.business.qld.gov.au

Statistics Information
www.abs.gov.au or www.ourbrisbane.com

Survey your Clients Free, using
www.surveymonkey.com

Research Web Keywords
www.google.com.au/services

Free Listing of Google Maps
http://maps.google.com.au

Free Business Listings
www.truelocal.com.au

85 Accepting Praise

Personal Development

Okay, praise first, this should be easy, but many people find it hard to accept praise. It can be embarrassing and often the response is to make some negative comment like, "oh, this old thing, it doesn't suit me". Instead, just smile and say "thanks". It's that simple. Enjoy the compliment and remember to take the opportunity to return a compliment. Ensure it is genuine and can be something as simple as saying to a co-worker "that colour suits you" or "Shane, you handled that call really well—I couldn't have done it better myself".

86 Accepting Criticism

Personal Development

Okay, this one is harder. Naturally we don't like to be criticised, so try this:

- Recognise in business or in the workplace, that the criticism is about the job performed, or the product supplied. It is not about you as a person. Now, on rare occasions, the criticism might be personal, such as, you have a body odour problem and need to use a deodorant.
- Try to step back and look at the criticism objectively. Is what they are saying correct and reasonable, and could you do better?
- Think of criticism as an opportunity for personal or business improvement and development. If a client says to me, "Donna I tried six times to reach your office on the phone, but kept getting an engaged signal" then this is a criticism, but it is also an opportunity for me to consider that I might need another incoming line. If I do install another line, clients will not have problems ringing into my office and I

will have happier clients and not deter any potential new clients that otherwise may have given up.

- Thank the person for the feedback. If bosses, clients and even staff know they can give criticism or feedback without being growled at, then they will. Remember the prior point; it is an opportunity to improve. Be thankful they feel they can communicate with you and not simply take their business elsewhere.
- As a business, document feedback, think about what you can do to improve and possibly change your systems or processes (for example, adding a phone line) to improve your business. There is always room for improvement!

87 Delivering Criticism

Personal Development

Now to the delivery—this is what you should do:

- Firstly, find something positive to cover before you introduce criticism.
- Then clearly define what was not done right or how what they are doing is not what you are looking for in your business. The criticism should be **positive!**
- Then provide advice or suggestions on how they could do it better.
- Give the recipient the opportunity to respond or ask questions.
- Finish on a positive note, particularly reinforcing what they did right.
- Do not shout, make personal digs or be emotional. If you are angry, then do not address the issue now, revisit it once you have calmed down.
- If it is serious, it may be wise to involve another person; either your business partner or the person's supervisor,

but first discuss your objective. Remember the point of the discussion is to improve the person, not to degrade them or make them feel so bad they want to quit.

- And if it was quite a serious infringement, or you suspect you may have to terminate that person down the track if it happens again, follow up with a written warning, outlining the basics of the meeting; what the problem was, what you will do to improve the situation, what they have agreed to do to improve and possibly set a follow up review time. Do not make the memo threatening, but do be clear regarding what you expect, so there is no room for a statement down the track such as "but I didn't know".

- Finally, do not deliver bad news or a criticism via email. Rousing on someone via email is just not wise and often can blow up and become far more serious than the initial problem.

88 Recommended Further Reading

Personal Development

No, I don't have a deal with other authors (but there's an idea!) but I certainly have gained a lot from others, so here are some of the books I can thoroughly recommend which you will get great value from—feel free to check out these titles:

- *Chicken Soup for the Soul*—by Jack Canfield and Mark Victor Hansen
- *E-Myth*—by Michael Gerber
- *How to Win Friends and Influence People*—by Dale Carnegie
- *Losing My Virginity*—by Richard Branson
- *Maximising Your Franchise*—by Glenn Walford (including guest writer Donna Stone)
- *Power Thoughts*—365 Daily Affirmations—by Louise L. Hay
- *Rich Dad Poor Dad*—by Robert Kiyosaki

- *The 7 Habits of Highly Effective People*—by Stephen R Covey
- *The Definitive Book of Body Language*—by Allan and Barbara Pease
- *Think and Grow Rich*—by Napoleon Hill
- *Time Management from the Inside Out*—by Julie Morgenstern
- *Who Moved my Cheese*—by Spencer Johnson

Processes & Procedures

"All things are difficult before they are easy".

—*John Norley*

INTRODUCTION TO PROCESSES & PROCEDURES

So why wouldn't we work out what a good process is, that which is easy and to set it as the pattern of how we do things? Why re-invent the wheel over and over and let each person doing a task be forced to learn the hard way? Having processes and procedures removes the 'trial and error' phase and you, your team and those who succeed them, can start from day one doing it the "easy" way and the right way.

89 Why Process and Systems are Valuable

Processes & Procedures

Okay, I know some people are systems people by nature and well, others just like to fly by the seat of their pants and "wing it". Sorry guys, if you are running a business, then I believe you have to have systems and procedures in place, especially if you plan to have more than one person in the team, besides yourself. Yes, whilst it is just you, you might make it work but as soon as you introduce other people you need to have systems, processes and procedures. Why, you ask? Having (especially documented) procedures in place will:

- Ensure things are done consistently every time
- Ensure nothing is forgotten
- Ensure all team members know the process or system
- Make it easier for new team members to learn the system.

90 How well do you Plan?

Here is a simple test to see how well you plan.

DIRECTIONS: FOR EACH QUESTION, CIRCLE THE NUMBER
THAT BEST DESCRIBES YOU

	Never	Seldom	Sometimes	Often	Always
How often do you plan in an effort to keep life from running out of control?	1	2	3	4	5
Do you put daily plans on paper?	1	2	3	4	5
Do you allow flexibility in your plans?	1	2	3	4	5
How often do you accomplish all you plan for a given day?	1	2	3	4	5
How often do you plan time for what matters most to you?	1	2	3	4	5
How often is your daily plan destroyed by urgent interruptions?	5	4	3	2	1

SCORING: Add the numbers next to your answers.

INTERPRETATION:

6-10: Terrible planner.
You should consider using new tools and processes to help you plan effectively. A great first step would be to take a time management course.

11-15: Below average planner.
You may already have a planning system, but using it more effectively will help to reduce the stress and lack of control you feel in your life.

16-20: Average planner.
Your planning system is working, but you can do better. You may need help focusing on priorities, dealing with urgent interruptions or writing your daily plan.

21-25: Above-average planner.
Your planning system is working well. Keep up the good work, with periodic reviews to be sure you are planning around what matters most in your life.

26-30: Excellent planner—or candidate for burnout?
You have mastered planning and should experience the serenity that comes from taking charge of your life. But make sure you are in control of your planning rather than letting it control you.

Quiz written for USA WEEKEND by time management expert Hyrum Smith, chairman of the Franklin Covey Co., whose Franklin Planners, agendas and planning software are used by 15 million Americans.

91

Have an Office Document that Spells it all Out

As above, have an office document that states how everything is done. An example of archiving is below. Try to be clear and precise so once someone is shown once, they can refer to the document thereafter for refreshing. Below is an example:

Archiving

- Archiving is done once a month to clean out the filing cabinets.
- Pull out any large or fat files and take out paperwork from the back (oldest), leaving at least the most current three months in the folder. Do not break financial years or financial quarters.
- Return the "thinned" folder back to its place in the active files.
- Put the old paperwork withdrawn into an old manila folder (recycling where possible).
- Write on the front of the folder what is in it (business name and time period—i.e. Smith Family Trust—July 2010 to June 2011). Then write also on the side of the folder.
- Select the next box number (if starting a new one) from the archive list. Ensure a box number is used only once (for example, you can't have two boxes with # 28)
- Add all items being archived to the list under that box number. The archive list is found at: My Documents/Administration/Archive New
- Whilst putting the items in the box, write on the front of the folder the box number i.e. (28)
- As you place items in the box, ensure they are standing upright on their side spine.
- Once the box is full, print out the list (for that box number) and stick it to the broad side of box. Stick the box number on the front of the box (printed in size 300 font). Every box has a contents list and number.
- Tell Donna via email that the box is complete and can be moved into the roof for storage.

92

Quality Assurance is not just a Waste of Money—there are Strong Benefits

Processes & Procedures

Quality Assurance (QA) is about having and documenting systems and processes to ensure that a certain quality is maintained. You can have a formal QA system which is fully audited and meets industry standards, or you may choose to adopt some of the concepts of QA into your business without the full formal process. The first step is to prepare your QA policy and document (type) it. You need to prepare the QA Policy. You can pay a professional (up to $10K in some cases) to do this for you or you can do it yourself. I strongly recommend that whichever way you go, you do not just accept a "shelf template" from a consultant. These systems, to be most effective, should be based around **your** business. Using someone else's processes does not mean you have a system customised to your business and therefore it may not be as beneficial. Once it is implemented and tested, you then have to continue using it. This means using forms, instigating processes that assure quality and then updating the plan and possibly undergoing audits. This all takes time and ultimately money, but in my experience QA actually can save you money!!

Here is a real life example which occurred in about 1995 when I was working for a small builder. In order to gain Government tenders the builder needed to have QA, so we instigated this according to ISO standards. One of the processes implemented regarding tenders, was that his figures were to be counter checked by another person. His tender take off sheet was about 20 pages long and one particular day, when adding up his figures he missed the total off an entire page. This page was the foundations/concrete, so was worth about $60K (going back 15 years . . . so heaps more now). This amount was well in excess of the profit margin. Because the QA process picked this up, the correct tender amount was submitted. We secured that job on the higher amount; but had we won it on the lower amount, we would have run that six month project at a loss!! This is a classic example of where QA literally paid for itself, by ten-fold.

Of course, by having a quality service, it means less mistakes are made and we all know that correcting mistakes costs us money in business—doing it right the first time, even a little slower, saves us money and saves our reputation and customer/client goodwill.

93 Having set Policies and Procedures in the Workplace is Beneficial

Processes & Procedures

I should also mention how staff like to know where they stand. So when you review or set up your policies, be sure to:

- be general enough so as to encompass all, but also give examples to explain clearly
- use simple language and clearly define what is to happen
- explain the background or why the policy is required
- outline when the policy applies, to whom and the consequences if it is ignored

Policy documents should not just be written and printed and left to stand in the corner, or never be updated. I believe these are 'living documents' which constantly evolve, grow and even change as needs arise. It may be that a certain system does not work well, so if it is agreed that something else works better, change the policy and advise all involved. Policy documents should cover a multitude of subjects including (but not only):

- how to answer the phone
- what to do if there is bullying
- how to handle a customer complaint
- what to do if you are sick and cannot get to work

- how to do a particular task, such as opening the mail or shipping a product
- how you speak to customers
- how to apply for annual leave
- personal use of internet and emails
- financial record security
- document backups
- filing
- confidentiality
- resigning
- petty cash
- honesty and theft
- completing timesheets
- workplace health and safety
- and much, much more.

These documents do take time to develop and grow, so do not expect to create one overnight, but also don't always put it off until 'tomorrow' as I can assure you, it will probably never happen. Remember, these documents have multiple purposes:

- they tell your staff clearly what is expected of them
- they give your staff confidence (and comfort) that they know the rules
- they give you substantiation if your staff do the wrong thing; they cannot plead ignorance
- they ensure things are done correctly
- they cut back on induction and training time; you don't have to repeat the details over and over every time someone new starts working for your business
- they improve your business; if your staff are doing things right, then your business will flow more smoothly and fewer mistakes will be made.

If you have more than three staff, now is the time to start this document; because as you grow, you will really reap the benefits.

94

Ensure you Always Backup Critical Data

Processes & Procedures

Have you created a "Disaster Plan" or done a SWOT analysis, where you have reviewed your weaknesses? A Disaster Plan, very simply is considering what could possibly happen to your business in a disaster and what plans you have in place to get back up on your feet? It might be an earthquake, or possibly a power strike, or a deadly computer virus. It might be a change in Government policy or a fire in your shop, office or premises. Whilst this stuff if pretty scary and could spell the end of your business, I know that if you consider the worse case scenarios and then sit down and seriously consider how you could prevent them, you will end up in a much better place. Let's use the example of a computer virus. You are a computer-based business and a virus wiping out your computer, network or server would be deadly. So, what will you do to prevent this happening? Great virus protection is one step. An offsite backup is another. Think about what could go wrong, and how you will prevent that situation or at least minimise the damage. It is a little like insurance, you hope you never need it, but don't you feel just a little bit more comfortable knowing you have it.

95

Have your Documents and Files Organised— a Filing Systems which Works for you

Processes & Procedures

I cannot tell you the best filing system to have. Every business is different. What I can suggest is keep it simple and be consistent. Colour coding often works well. Possibly having one Administration Cabinet and one Clients Cabinet might be an option. Put all your Admin issues in one cabinet, filed simply according to the alphabet, i.e. Advertising & Marketing, Banking, Computer Maintenance, Insurances, Staff Files, and Warranties etc. Simply have a suspension folder with the crystalline tab "Advertising" and put all your advertising material in there that you need to keep. File the most recent at the front. For your clients you may have a client file for each of your clients, and just file them alphabetically.

I suggest you keep your "Bills Paid" paperwork separate again. Just a simple lever arch file, with the description and date range on it. Inside have PVC or cardboard dividers (either alpha or date orientated) and file accordingly.

Set up a simple system which will work, and then you can delegate that task to someone else to do. **Do not let it build up.** I cannot stress this enough. Rummaging through a pile of papers over and over is so time wasteful; if you had just filed it initially, you would save so much time. Delegate the filing task out. Possibly a mum with school aged children wanting a few hours of work a week, or a senior high school student for an afternoon a week after school or even a retired person just wanting a little something to keep them active. Remember, the concept of delegating and consider the benefits of having a neatly filed office AND you not doing it, so that you can "work on the business, not in it".

96 How to Plan Your Week—Default Diary

Processes & Procedures

Before you plan your week, you need to consider:

- Defining your objectives. What are your goals? What do you need to do to achieve these goals? Having a clear defined objective here will help alleviate vague drifting.
- Analyse the use of your time. Sit down and think about how you spend your time. Are you a person who jumps from task to task, gets a million interruptions and then has to waste time looking for something in a pile you need? If

so, read the section on time management, that will help. Once you know where you spend your time, then you can choose if you want to change that and how.

- Plan and Note. Now is the time to start your plan . . . what are you going to do at certain times. For example, I often do all my networking and new client meetings on a Tuesday. I have client appointments on a Thursday and staff training on a Friday morning. This way for example, I am out of the office Tuesdays and Thursdays, so my travel is minimised and I am focused on those tasks that day. You might allocate one hour each morning for checking and answering emails and another half hour mid afternoon. You might set aside think time, or time to read business magazines.
- Action and Review. Once your plan is in place, things do change. That client you absolutely want to land rings for an appointment. You try the Tuesday and Thursday, but they are out of town until Friday noon and leave again on the weekend, so of course you schedule the appointment on Friday afternoon. Plans are there as guidelines, but they also need to be flexible.

97 How to Plan Your Day

Processes & Procedures

- Firstly, try to do your planning at the same time every day. It might be over that first cup of coffee in the morning, or as soon as you walk in the door, even before you turn on the computer and check out the new batch of emails.
- Whilst we often hear the phrase "don't mix business with pleasure", I absolutely suggest you keep just one planner or diary for your entire life. If you have a specialist appointment at 9am in your private diary and then book a client at 9am in your work diary it is just not going to work.

- Review your default weekly diary. Let's say it is a Monday in which you are scheduled to work in the office.
- As you complete tasks on your "To Do List" mark them off. I use a blue highlighter and it is so satisfying to have "blued" out all my tasks by the end of the day.
- Diarise time to do special activities. You might have three quotes to prepare. Block off the morning as an "appointment" so you do not book in anything else, and hit those quotes with a vengeance.
- Next you might have a Task List. Things you know you need to do that day. I suggest you do not be overly ambitious with this list. It is amazing how only three tasks can sometimes take a full day. Remember you are in the office, so are likely to receive phone calls, emails etc, and this all takes time. Whilst you may plan only to action three tasks, and answer emails for one hour, be prepared that unplanned things will also just occur. Perhaps a machine breaks down, or a new client spends an hour on the phone with you talking about their needs. Whilst you must plan, also plan for the unexpected.
- Some people say to prioritise your task list. I don't, I just suggest that you keep it short and the objective is that you do it all. When I go to add items to my daily task lists, I look at what is already there. If tomorrow has four items already, I will either add it to today, or the day after tomorrow—just spreading it out so that there are an achievable number of items on each day.
- Hit the worst item on your task list first. It's like the concept of eating the least favourite vegetable off your dinner plate first. Get it out of the way and then the rest of the items feel easier and often are and you will whip through them. Leaving the hardest or least pleasing item until last really just adds weight to that activity.

Sales & Marketing

"If you are not taking care of your customer, your competitor will."

—*Bob Hooey*

"Nobody raises his own reputation by lowering others"

—*Anonymous*

INTRODUCTION TO SALES & MARKETING

For many of us, as business owners and operators we have to either wear this hat ourselves, or find someone to wear the hat. Most businesses at one point or another need to market, promote and sell their products or services, whether you are selling a product, tendering, quoting or out there spreading the word about your business.

98 Surround Yourself with People Better than you

Sales & Marketing

This tip does not just apply to marketing, it relates to many aspects of your business. It might be about having a great accountant, quality bookkeeper, switched on legal eagle or a marketing expert.

Be realistic. You are in business and let's say you are an electrician. You are most likely an excellent sparkie, know your trade well and might even consider yourself an expert in your trade. But are you just as good at bookkeeping, marketing or law? Quite likely not! So why would you try to do your marketing, develop your marketing plan or write your advertisements? Don't. Get an expert in who is better than you, who knows this stuff and can do it better, quicker and more effectively than you can. You do what you do well; let others do what they do well, even if it is a task which is working "on" your business.

99

Work ON the Business, not IN the Business

This leads me to my next point. We have all heard the expression "work on your business, not in your business" but I am amazed at how many business owners fail to do this, and especially new business owners. I particularly see it with bookkeeping. One new business operator I met when starting out decided she would do her books herself. She is intelligent and figured she could save a dollar.

So a year on, I received a call from her. Help! She had done the books for the first year, sent them to the Accountant and he was not a 'happy chappy'. He had to spend a heap of time fixing up the work which meant a larger accounting bill. So a year later, she contacted me to get that training and assistance I had offered a year earlier. And what about all that time over the last year that she had spent slaving over the books, when instead she could have been focusing on growing her business? Here are a list of tasks and classification of each. Count up how many you do in each category and really give this some thought, particularly if you want to grow your business and make some money.

WORKING **ON** THE BUSINESS TASKS	WORKING **IN** THE BUSINESS TASKS
Networking	Providing services to clients/customers
Sales and Marketing activities	Bookkeeping
Learning and self development	Administration
Meeting with new clients	Emailing (unless it is, for example, marketing)
Setting up processes and procedures	Cleaning or tidying up
Planning (re your business, goals etc)	Invoicing customers
Review of financial performance	Teaching/training/supervising your staff
Meeting with your business coach	Handling client enquiries

100 Research your Idea/Business/Concept Before You Start

Sales & Marketing

Before you jump head on into an idea or concept or business, remember that to do it properly you are going to invest a good amount of your time and money into this venture. If you were going to buy a house, you would inspect it, check out what else is available, have it inspected by a builder, ask questions about it and generally fully evaluate your purchase. You should do the same before starting a new business venture. Over the years, I have seen wide-eyed business adventurers with massive enthusiasm for a concept, which of course their loved ones say is a wonderful idea, invest a fortune to later achieve failure. On a brief introduction to their concept, I have seen huge holes in their idea—and all those that failed did not take the time to research it properly. Some things you need to look at are:

- is there a demand for your product or service?
- does the product or service serve a need?
- will others buy it?
- does value exceed cost?

And please, do not research this emotionally. Do not limit your research to your best friends or family. Approach those who might be your target market and ask them for an honest response. It is better to spend a few hours/days researching, than a few hundred thousand dollars failing.

101 Dress the Part

Any good salesperson or marketing book will tell you how important packaging is. Does your product look good, smell good, feel good etc. Do not forget that you, as an individual, business operator, or even a staff member, are part of the packaging. Do your staff have neat and tidy uniforms? Or do they turn up to work in jeans, thongs or low cut tops? Do you turn up to clients' offices in a suit, business outfit or casual trousers and a sweat shirt? Again it certainly depends on what your business is, and obviously if you have a lawn mowing business, you will not wear a suit, but looking professional, for your profession, is important.

An accountant who I was consulting with had excellent knowledge and skills but a rather casual approach, including her choice of clothing. I reminded her that she should dress the part and she admitted to me later I was right. She had been working for a bookkeeping client for over a year and always dressed very casually when meeting with the client. One day she had a second appointment in the city in a solicitor's office, so was dressed up when she met with the usual client beforehand. For the first time, that client saw her as the Accountant she really was and asked her to do an accounting job for them in addition to her bookkeeping functions. They suddenly perceived her professional skill and experience purely because she *looked* professional. People perceive that if you take pride in your appearance, then you take pride in your work.

102 Speak the Part

Sales & Marketing

Most business owners are also sales people. This means you need to be able to speak properly and often present—either to a small group or sometimes quite a large forum. If you are not a good public speaker, then I strongly recommend that you take some time to develop this skill. There are many training organisations that specifically train people for public speaking. Even if you do not do this, I suggest at least you:

- Pre-plan what you are going to say—do not just "wing it".
- Practice, practice, practice.
- Do not read your piece, learn it and just have dot point reminder notes.
- Inject humour where you can.
- Be yourself.
- Do not try to cover too much. Less is best.

103

Open your Mouth and Spread the Word

Sales & Marketing

Forget the phrase "quiet achiever" if you want to get more business. You have to be out there telling people you exist and what you do, and how you (or your product) will be beneficial to them. Sell yourself!! It does not have to be the 'hard sell', just let people know you are there and wanting business. We know that less than 10% of job vacancies are advertised; most jobs are filled through word or mouth or direct application. Whilst I do not know the specifics for business leads, I do know in my own business, 89% of our new work is from word of mouth. It is a powerful thing so be sure to use it. Sure, some businesses, such as a white goods rental business, will find that advertisements with Yellow Pages is the most effective means, but other businesses will find that spreading the word is the trick. Use a number of marketing means, but always remember the value of word of mouth.

104

Track your Business Leads

Sales & Marketing

When a prospective new client rings you, do you *always* ask how they heard of you? You absolutely should, and then of course note this down. Keep a statistical database, sheet, or listing. It can even be really simple—just have a page where you have say ten boxes for the different ways someone could get on to you (i.e. yellow pages advert, staff, friends, associates, marketing mail-out, web page etc) and put a tick for each time a lead comes from that direction. Once you know where the leads are coming from, you will know what marketing methods are not working and what are working. If you spend $10K per annum on magazine advertising that generates one lead per year, then I for one would be dumping that specific advertising. If spending one hour a week at a networking function generates three leads, then keep going, or better yet, go to two functions a week. And take note of those who 'sing your praises' and tell others about your business and remember to reward them. In fact, that can be one of your strategies. When you send or give a product to a customer, have a voucher in their package that offers them something free when they refer a friend. Maybe they will get a discount, or free gift as a token of your thanks. The gift may cost you $20, but what is the new client worth to your business, particularly factoring in repeat sales?

105 Grade your Clients and Have an Annual Cull

Sales & Marketing

You should grade your clients A, B, C & D. The A grade client, gives you lots of business, is easy to deal with, has reasonable expectations, pays on time and even better, promotes your products and services to others. They are excellent clients and be sure you are looking after them.

Now let's talk about your D grade client. They don't spend much with you, but you expend excess energy dealing with them. They have unrealistic demands, are difficult, cause your staff stress, never pay on time and even have the audacity to get cranky when you ring and request payment. So do you *really* want this type of client?

Now you might say to me, times are tough; I need more clients—so I might have to put up with them for the moment. Are you sure? Imagine you cull (ditch) the D grade client. Now you have room for a new client (who if you are lucky or screen well, might be an A or B grade client. Alternatively, with this saved time, you might be able to give your current A or B grade clients more of your time and nurture them more. The D grade client is not doing your business any good—so lose them. It might be an annual cull, or quarterly review or just when you've had enough. But do not react in the heat of the moment, do this calmly and be firm.

There are a number of tactics to ditch a client; perhaps a mail out advising you are not longer servicing their type of business, or a personal call, saying it is not working, or an increase in rates (for that client only) which either will lose them, or otherwise they are paying 'nuisance' money and this makes working with them less painful. I once had a D grade client who never gave us the paperwork, never paid his bill on time (in fact often dragged it out twelve months), and often complained, but when I tried to ask to him to leave, he refused to go. I tried rate increases, which (after complaining) he accepted and then finally, I put my foot down and said he would have to pre-pay for his service or go. At last, he left. He argued that he had given me $20K worth of business over the years (true) but I didn't point out that he regularly owed me $10K at any one time and was not paying interest at the time (I know better now), so in fact, all I was to him was a free bank. It can be hard, so you will need to be firm and determined; if you are unsure, they will sense it (if they want to stay) and grind you down into allowing them to stay (and continue with the bad habits). My experience is that if you give someone a chance to change their ways, if they don't after one chance, there is no point giving them a second, third or fourth chance. They are set in their ways and really won't (or can't) change. Accept this and move on.

Customer Complaints

Your first step is to listen. Look attentive and listen. If you need to write notes or clarify, do so, but initially spend most of your time listening. This will do two things. Firstly, it will allow the other person to vent. They need to do this. It will also inform you of what the situation is. You need to know what has happened. It is really important that you have a good attitude about complaints. Think of complaints as an opportunity. This is an opportunity to improve and do things better. Do not just assume that it is someone whinging and have a closed mind before you even start.

Encourage the person and do not argue. Stand in their shoes and try to imagine how you would feel. Would you be upset or annoyed in this situation?

Thank them for their time in giving you this feedback or letting you know. Many people do not complain, they simply action their dissatisfaction by using their feet and taking their business elsewhere. This is also an opportunity of not just possibly improving your service, but also of retaining this client or customer. How you handle this complaint WILL absolutely have a direct affect on whether you keep the client. Remember that 68% of clients/customers move from a business due to indifference (or perceived indifference). Well, now is the time to not be indifferent.

Once you know what the problem is, then ascertain what you can do to fix it. Now this might mean re-doing a piece of work, or giving them a replacement product, or passing the matter on to a higher level. Whatever it is, be pleasant, and be sure to tell the person what you will do. Then be sure to do it.

On a final note, you do not have to accept abuse. If someone swears at you or yells at you, then ask them to stop. If they refuse (and it is a phone call), advise them that if they do not cease abusing you, you will hang up, and then do so.

We know the expression "you can't please all the people all the time" . . . well there are some people you can never please. Do what you can, but at the end of the day, if someone simply cannot be pleased or they are not reasonable, you just have to walk away.

107 Write Advertisements which Sell

Sales & Marketing

I am NOT a marketing expert, but I have picked up a few tips from those who are. The first and foremost is to write advertisements which are about my customer, not about me (or you in this case). Rather than telling them that I have x years experience, that I have a professional manner, or that I have certain qualifications, instead I tell them how I will be the solution to **their** need. Word your advertisement with regard to how they will benefit, how their challenges will be resolved and how they will feel as a result of dealing with my business.

108 Have a "Kick-ass" Heading

Sales & Marketing

Having your business name as the heading or in large print is a waste of money, unless you are Coke, Microsoft or some other massive conglomerate. Whilst as a business owner, your ego might feel good seeing your name in large print . . . you are wasting your advertising space. Often asking a critical question in the heading is effective, such as "Does your bookkeeping stress you?" Or a finance broker came up with "What would you spend $40,000 on?" which is what they had saved a client by switching their finance.

Have a heading which is catchy and reaches people. You have to snag your reader with your heading—otherwise the advertisement will likely be a total waste of money.

109 Pain or Pleasure?

Sales & Marketing

Most sales are based on either pain or pleasure. Most of us are providing either a product which will give pleasure, such as a luxurious red convertible BMW Roadster, or the other angle is that we are relieving a pain—it might be the pain of completing your bookkeeping correctly so as to avoid a painful tax audit. Consider how your product or service could remedy or relieve a specific pain or problem experienced by a prospective client; or could provide them with pleasure or enhance their business or personal life. And interestingly, pain is the stronger emotion, over pleasure.

110 Call to Action

Sales & Marketing

A call to action is telling the reader what you want them to do and when. It might be "Call today for a free quote" or "Register before 31st March to receive the bonus three hour consultation". In other words, your aim is to elicit from the reader a positive and timely response to your offer.

111

Make it Easy for People to do Business with you

Sales & Marketing

This sounds basic, but often people who want us to use their product or service make it so hard for us to do so. One really good example is a workshop I wanted to attend. I received the email and wanted to attend but "simply register" turned out to be so hard, so painful and so difficult that they lost me.

On the other hand, a recent workshop I attended had such a fantastically easy process, that I had registered in about four seconds. The email had a "register" button, which essentially was an automatic return email. I simply typed in my name, company, email address and phone number and hit "send" and it was done. AND they emailed me a tax invoice within seconds along with a lovely warm welcoming email. They made it so easy for me to do business with them. Many people are time starved, impatient or do not have the computer skills of a programmer to navigate the challenges of a complicated system, so remember the good old fashioned KISS principle—Keep it simple sweetheart.

- 128 -

Social Media

"The miracle of this—the more we share, the more we have".

—*Leonard Nimoy (Actor)*.

Being a Trekkie, I had to include this quote, but it's true, I think social media is all about sharing. D.

INTRODUCTION TO SOCIAL MEDIA

Throughout this book you will hear me talk about delegating and surrounding yourself with people who are better than you on subjects you don't know well. So, I took a leaf out of my own book and sought the advice of Julie, as I knew I was quite green on the subject of social media, which is such an emerging field. For the following chapter, I have the pleasure of introducing Julie Mason, whom I have often referred to as a "social media guru".

Julie Mason

Social Media Consultant, Author / Speaker

Julie Mason operates a consultancy company that guides businesses to build an engaging and profitable presence on Facebook, Twitter, LinkedIn and YouTube as well as providing 'Done-For-You' services.

Prior to her work helping businesses with their online marketing, Julie worked for over 15 years helping companies grow using more traditional offline methods of sales and marketing. Her customers included Brisbane Airport, BHP Billiton, Gold Coast City Council, The Construction Industry Unions of NSW & ACT, Ericsson and Myer, just to name a few.

Realising the potential of the internet, Julie completed extensive education in web design, affiliate-marketing, pay per click advertising, search engine optimisation and social media. With her wealth of knowledge in offline sales and marketing she is able to help clients build their online marketing message that will generate leads and profits for your business.

Julie is offering a 30 day FREE trial of *Social Media Success* membership program. To claim your FREE trial simply visit the website to register at www.TheSocialMediaPrincess.com.

112 Get a Positive Social Media Attitude

Social Media

Do you roll your eyes when you hear people talk about Facebook?
Laugh when you hear someone mention Twitter?
Think Blogs are something found in a Pixar Animated Movie?
View YouTube as just a place to watch funny videos?
Thought LinkedIn was a band?

OR

Are you actively posting on Facebook and engaging with users?
Tweeting on relevant topics on Twitter?
Posting or commenting on Blogs?
Using YouTube videos to leverage your brand awareness?
Actively involved in LinkedIn to connect business to business?

Social media is not a "fad internet thing" that will disappear; it is a growing online community that is changing the way people interact with businesses and each other. Businesses that fail to understand this and do not tap into social media marketing are potentially missing out on extra business that could mean the difference between increased revenues or going broke.

113

This IS about Business too!

More and more businesses are starting to realise the value of tapping into social media to:

- Generate exposure for their business
- Drive traffic to their website/opt-in list/other
- Find new business partnerships
- Help raise their search engine ranking
- Generate qualified leads
- Sell products or services
- Reduce overall marketing expenses

Businesses that successfully utilise social media marketing usually employ a number of different approaches rather than just relying on one approach. Combining more than one approach gives you the opportunity for even more market exposure.

Word of mouth marketing is now really ***world of mouth*** marketing. Instead of people recommending or even complaining about your business to a few friends, they now have the power to send recommendations or complaints to everyone in their social media network within seconds.

If you are of the belief that people are not talking on social media about the services and products that they use, then you are seriously mistaken. People are having "brand" conversations whether you are aware of them or not.

114

The Highway Hotel, South Australia

Tom Williamson who does the marketing and communications for the hotel first started engaging in social media marketing in October 2009. Their key strategy is to consistently engage their followers on a daily basis and encourage them to interact with the hotel's online profile.

Within twelve months, The Highway gained more than 10,000 fans on Facebook and over 1,400 followers on Twitter. Their Facebook page includes their menus, upcoming events, photos and special meal offers. They saw the benefit of 'Foursquare', a location-based application used via mobile phones and quickly developed a "check-in" special for The Highway. By creating a special "check-in" offer it not only entices guests to visit the hotel but encourages them to tell their friends as well.

Williamson says that using social media, which is free, has saved the hotel over $15,000 in marketing costs over a nine-month period. "The Highway's turnover increased by four per cent. This can be attributed to many things," said Williamson "but social media is certainly a major contributing factor." (Sourced from www. smh.com.au, August 24, 2010).

So, let's have a closer look at these different social networks in order to understand how they work, best business practices and some secret tips.

Facebook

- **Over 500 million active users on Facebook**
- 50% of users log on to Facebook in any given day
- **People spend over 700 billion minutes on Facebook every month**
- More than 70% of users are outside the United States
- **Average user has 130 friends and is connected to 80 community pages, groups or events**
- The largest increase of users on Facebook are aged between 35-49 years old
- **There are over 900 million objects that people can interact with such as pages, groups, events and community pages**

115 There are Four Different types of Pages on Facebook

Social Media

It is important to know which page is appropriate when looking at using Facebook for business and the difference between the pages.

1. Personal Page
   By having a personal account you can interact with the global Facebook community, add friends, view and like pages, join groups, message people, share content, and generally build your personal profile.

2. Like Page (previously known as a Fan Page)
   A Like page is designed for promotion of businesses, services, products or celebrity profiles. While it can be created without having a personal account the downside is access is somewhat

limited with other Facebook pages and people. If created through your personal profile account, your personal identity will be kept private and any posts that you send will appear in the name the Page is given when created.

3. Group Page
   Groups can be created by any user and about any topic. They can be open to the public or accessible only to invitees. When posting on the Group Page your personal identity will be shown next to each post you write as the Group's creator. However, unlike a Like Page, a Group administrator has the ability to send a message to all the members of the Group.

4. Community Page
   These are a new type of Page that enables you to see what people are saying about the things that matter to you and discover people who share these connections with you. However, they will not generate stories in your News Feed and are not maintained by a single author. They will often have an information section from Wikipedia at the beginning of the Page.

116 If you are not Already on Facebook, you are Behind the Eight—ball

Social Media

It is time to get started on your social media journey and the best way to start is to learn the basics. Sign up on www.facebook.com. Use Facebook's Friend Finder and connect with people you know already, use the search box at the top of the Facebook page and research what other companies are doing with their marketing. Take a look at those who are doing it successfully such as Starbucks (with over 13 million followers), Zappos (with over 64,000 followers) and see how they engage their customers with their marketing.

117

Work out a Strategy to Engage People

Social Media

You cannot afford to just "have a stab" at social media and hope that you get it right. It is important to have a planned strategy and that you are aware of the level of commitment you need to give in order to generate results. Facebook users are well known for turning against companies that do not uphold their promises and once you lose their trust it is very difficult to gain it back.

118

When Building a Facebook Like Page never let First-time Users Land on your Wall

Social Media

You want to engage visitors to your Page from the moment they arrive and the best way to do so is to have a special landing page that encourages them to click the LIKE button, engage and share the page with their friends. There are many ways to encourage them from simple text comments through inserting images or graphics—check out BMW's Welcome tab on Facebook as a good example.

119

Ensure that You are Consistent with Your Dialogue

Social Media

It doesn't matter if you are having a conversation on Facebook, Twitter, LinkedIn, your Blog or your doing a presentation; it is important that you keep to your message theme. It is okay to be involved with different conversations but remember to keep the bulk of your conversations to your message theme. To give an example, Bill Gates would not have a conversation with software developers about beauty tips, just like Oprah would not have a conversation with her viewers about computer programming. Therefore it is important that your conversation be consistent with your customers.

120 Cross—promote

Social Media

Make sure there is a link to your website on your Facebook page—whether it is on the Info tab or in the mini-bio area under the profile picture or ideally, both. Put a link on your website that gives people the option to "Like" your Facebook page and to follow you on Twitter or LinkedIn. This helps with your search engine optimisation as well, both for your website and your Facebook page. Remember to add a link to your different social media pages at the bottom of all out-going emails, letting all your customers know that you have a page on Facebook so that they can choose to engage and follow you online.

121 Post Rich Content to Engage Interest

Social Media

Rich content includes videos, pictures and links that are relevant and interesting to your target market. There was a study done by Sysomos which found little correlation between how frequently the Facebook page admin posted on to the wall and the total number of followers but there <u>is</u> a correlation between the amount of other content such as notes, links, photos, videos, events and the total number of followers. So to really grow your business Facebook page following, make sure that your strategy involves posting rich content.

122 TAG—YOU'RE IT!

Remember the school-yard game of Tag? You spent the whole time trying not to get tagged. Well, to grow your Facebook profile and encourage people to interact, an ideal activity to do is to 'tag' people. Ensure you take photos of any events/workshops/ seminars or the like including photos of people you meet (with their permission of course) and upload them to your Facebook page. When the photo has uploaded you can click the link "Tag This Photo" and move the pointer to the person that you want to name in the photo then click and enter their name. When finished, click on 'Done Tagging'.

If the person you have tagged has a Facebook account they will receive a message saying that they have been tagged in your photo. It is another great way to interact and engage with people who follow you.

123 Go Mobile!

Mobile phones now are a standard accessory that people carry everywhere, so it should not be surprising that more than 150 million active users log into Facebook via their mobile phones every day. The important thing to take away from this snippet of information is that these users are twice as active in sharing and commenting on information posted on Facebook. Mobile Facebook users like to be connected and often have larger numbers of friends or followers making them good influencers in your network as they will share your information to a greater number of contacts if they are engaged with you or your Facebook page.

Twitter

- **Over 106 million registered accounts**
- Twitter users are sending over 55 million tweets per day—over 600 tweets per second
- **More than 300,000 new accounts are created daily**
- Thursday and Friday are the most active days on Twitter

124 How to set up your Twitter Account Correctly

Social Media

Start by joining up at www.twitter.com. It is quick and easy and they have a simple step-by-step guide to help you start using Twitter. As Twitter is search engine friendly it is really important to make sure your keywords, that describe your business, are in your Username and your Bio. To write a good Bio, include your keywords for your niche and mention what you do and include a link to your website.

If you have already set up your account and would like to change your Bio, simply click on Settings and then visit the 'Profile' tab and you can make any changes and then save. See the picture below . . .

Image courtesy of Twitter.com

125 — Make a Good First Impression

Social Media

First impressions count . . . even on Twitter. So make your first post impactful about who you are and what you do. For example,

> *Hi, Julie here from easyonlinemarketingforyou.com hoping to share great tips and ideas on #internet marketing and #social media for business*

Remember to use the hashtags to categorise the Tweet as well as introduce yourself to the Twitter community as shown above.

126

Are you a Twit or a Twitterer?

The fact is that most people just do not understand Twitter and the enormous potential it has to raise your business profile. This is supported by the fact that many accounts become inactive within 30 days of being opened. People can get overwhelmed with the lingo and not understand the flow of the conversation. So let's do a quick overview of the common Twitter lingo:

Tweet	is a post or update made up of a maximum 140 characters in length.
# or Hashtag	by putting a # before a keyword you will help to categorise your Tweets. If anyone then searches for that keyword in Twitter your post will then be categorised within the search results.
RT or ReTweet	often used where other individuals like a person's post and want to share it with their followers. This is done by clicking on the ReTweet sign underneath a post.
@username	to create a link to another person's username simply put the @ symbol directly before their name to create a link to that user's Twitter profile.
Follower	people who are following you on Twitter. Remember Twitter is a Relationship building tool—users follow others that they find Interesting.
Following	people you are following on Twitter. If you are new to Twitter, only follow a few people to start off with until you feel comfortable and understand

the flow of the conversation and how to interact and engage properly, then you can start following more people. If you follow too many people at the start you may feel overwhelmed and go inactive.

DM Direct Message. This allows private messages between Tweeters, generally only from followers or following users. Use this for passing private information like phone numbers, accounts or email addresses or information that you do not want visible in the public news stream.

127 Going, Going, Going . . . GONE!

Social Media

Using social media for business does not mean that the old traditional sales methods of SELL, SELL, SELL apply. In fact, selling is about the last activity that should be undertaken on social media. Social media platforms such as Twitter, Facebook and LinkedIn, if used correctly, can help position your business as the leader within the industry. However, try selling to users upfront and you will find yourself out in the cold very quickly. People want to know about who you are, what you do, what type of business you run and then they will ask their networks if anyone has done business with you and what their recommendations are . . . before they will put their trust in you to purchase your product or service.

128 ReTweet to build relationships

Social Media

The way to show someone that you like their message on Twitter is to ReTweet it and forward it through to your followers on your news stream. The person whose message you have forwarded along will appreciate your actions and often return the favour in kind by ReTweeting your messages that they find of value to themselves and their followers.

As you build up these relationships, your message will be spread to a wider and wider audience, that may in turn ReTweet your message even further afield.

129 Schedule Ahead

Too busy to get your Tweets posted but know what message you want to send out to your followers? Consider using a program that will schedule your Tweets for you and post them out at the times you specify throughout the day. Some good ones to consider are:

SocialOomph   Has a wide range of features including scheduling your Tweets

TwitResponse   Allows you to set up unlimited messages to be scheduled for delivery to your Twitter account

HootSuite   Not only allows you to schedule Tweets but can also send posts to multiple social media accounts at once thereby saving you time and energy

There are hundreds of these types of programs—look for one that integrates all your social media accounts such as HootSuite. This will save you time and allow you to be much more productive with your social media engagement.

130

Most Active Days on Twitter

Research has found that the most active days on Twitter are Thursday and Friday. This may mean that you will need to Tweet more on these days so that your Tweets stay higher on the Twitter news stream than on other days.

To find out what the best time of the day to Tweet so that your message is received and responded to, you will need to test and measure different times throughout the day and measure how many people respond or ReTweet your posts.

YouTube

- **People are watching 2 billion videos a day on YouTube**
- 51% of users go to YouTube weekly or more often
- **For every minute there is 24 hours of video uploaded to YouTube**
- 70% of YouTube's traffic comes from outside of the United States
- YouTube Video Consumption across the social networks:
  - **Facebook: 46.2 years of videos watched a day**
  - MySpace: 5.6 years of videos watched a day

131

Big or Small, In Fact, Any Size At All . . .

It doesn't matter if your business is big or small; YouTube provides the same benefits to everyone. Any type of business can benefit from using online videos whether it is a retail business, technology business or service business.

To set up a YouTube channel visit www.YouTube.com and on the top right hand side of the screen click Create Account. Follow the steps and you will have your very own online video channel in a matter of minutes. Remember to use your keywords (if possible) within your account name improving your search engine results.

Now you can use it to share your knowledge, demonstrate your products, offer helpful tips and connect with customers, colleagues or prospects.

132 How To Upload A Video

Social Media

There are two ways to upload videos to YouTube. Firstly, if you have video files already stored on your computer or on a disc, you simply click on Upload at the top of the screen and then select the yellow 'Upload Video' button and it will open up a new window so that you can select the file on your computer. Once you have found the file and selected it, click Open and it will start to automatically upload.

The second way to upload video is to click on Upload at the top of the screen and select "Record from Webcam". This, of course is only suitable if you have a webcam attached to your computer but beware that this is a live recording that will be uploaded. If you do not feel comfortable doing a live recording, perhaps you should pre-record your video using your webcam, save it to your computer and upload using the first option described above.

Whenever you upload a video make sure that you always fill in the description of what the video is about using your keywords again within that text and putting a link to your website such as http://www.mywebsite.com so that people can visit your site for more information.

1. Positioning yourself as an expert or thought-leader in your industry by:

   - Uploading recordings of presentations you have given
   - Creating short videos of valuable hints and tips that are of interest to your clients and prospects
   - Interview experts within your industry—attaching yourself to the experts as the interviewee will still provide you with positioning within your industry.

2. For marketing and advertising

   - Put together a creative video that explains your product or service
   - Ask your customers or clients for a video testimonial—this will add to your credibility with online prospective clients
   - Promote any of your upcoming events—don't forget to add some video footage of your previous events to add excitement
   - Take a video tour of your office, introduce your staff on video to help viewers feel connected to you
   - Always add your company information in every video including your website address, phone number and email address—this can be added in the description area when uploading your video
   - Put a link on your website to your YouTube Channel

3. For Customer Service

   - Create some "How To" videos to help customers who have purchased your products or services

- Post videos on commonly asked product or service questions or problems
- Add your videos to your website or blog posts where appropriate
- Add the closed-caption option to your videos (using 'Caption and Subtitles' menu on the editing page within your YouTube account) to help those who are hearing impaired

134 Sharing Your Videos on Facebook and Other Social Media sites

Social Media

The equivalent of over 46 years worth of YouTube videos are watched through Facebook accounts every day! It is amazing how many people interact with videos on Facebook compared to users on www.MySpace.com who watch just over 5 years worth of YouTube videos each day.

By posting your video onto your Facebook page it automatically adds it into the News Feeds of all those following you on Facebook and opens it up to being viewed by their connections as well. This gives much more exposure to your information and the opportunity to engage with a broader audience. However, even though Facebook users may view the most YouTube videos on a day-to-day basis, it is worthwhile posting them on all your social media accounts including putting a link to your video in Twitter posts.

135 Do not Tolerate Offensive Comments

Social Media

Whilst you need to deal with legitimate complaints or negative comments towards your product, service or business in a transparent manner, you can take a stand against offensive or spammy comments. This requires good judgement and it is obviously NOT a good idea to remove any negative or critical comments, especially relevant ones as this will show a lack of customer service and care towards your online followers.

You can certainly remove any comments with offensive language or containing spam messages. If you are challenged over the removal of those comments, it is best to make a simple statement to the effect that these types of comments will not be tolerated. Should the need arise, you have the option to block users that continue with unsocial behaviour, however, only as a last resort. You can nip this in the bud by changing your settings to 'Moderate' any comments before they are posted.

LinkedIn

> - **LinkedIn has over 75 million members in over 200 countries**
> - About half of the members on LinkedIn are outside of the United States
> - **A new member joins LinkedIn approximately every second**
> - Executives from all Fortune 500 companies are LinkedIn members

136 LinkedIn Is Not A Popularity Contest

Social Media

While LinkedIn is often referred to as the Facebook for professionals, it is not a popularity contest to see who can get the most contacts. Nor should it be treated as such. LinkedIn is however, a valuable resource, giving you access to people, jobs and other opportunities.

LinkedIn is also where you create your professional profile presenting your expertise and accomplishments to potential employers (and employees) as well as potential clients, joint venture partners or strategic alliances. As a network builder, LinkedIn gives you the ability to connect on a professional level with other people that may benefit your business in the future.

To set up your profile go to www.LinkedIn.com and enter your details, it's easy and free.

137 Hints to Developing a Strong Profile

Social Media

1. LinkedIn is not a resumé resource centre, it is a network of professional-minded people. So rather than cutting and pasting your resumé into your Profile, describe your experience and talents as you would to someone face to face, in a conversational manner.

2. Keep your paragraphs short—large blocks of text become hard to read and lose the interest of the reader.

3. Make your title work for you—it is the first thing people see in your profile so help it stand out and describe who you are; remember first impressions count.

4. Do not skip over the Summary! It is where you define who you are, what you do and why you are unique and most importantly, where you engage readers. Make it conversational and meaningful in order to gain more attention time from readers.

5. The 'Specialties' field is search engine friendly so it is important to add your keywords in this area. Any special interests, abilities or passions you have in your profession should be

showcased in this area allowing others a deeper insight to your Profile.

6. Again, rather than copying and pasting your resume for experience (both past and present), describe a bit about the company you represent/represented and what your role is/was within the company.

7. Change the default setting for "My Website" to show your website address (i.e. www.mywebsite.com.au). This will help with search engine rankings and encourage more traffic to your website.

8. Upload a Profile photo—try to keep your Profile photo the same across all the social media platforms, allowing people to recognise you more readily.

9. Recommendations are the key to strengthening your Profile on LinkedIn. Ask for recommendations from past employers, colleagues or people that you have done business with in the past and always return the favour.

10. Add an application to engage readers' interest such as the "Reading List by Amazon" application and select a few books that you are currently reading to be displayed. This is another great way to add depth to your Profile.

138 Join Some Groups

One of the best things on LinkedIn is the Group feature. If you are new to LinkedIn, I would suggest joining a few relevant industry groups to your business. To find out what Groups are available click on 'Groups' in the menu bar and select 'Groups Directory' from the drop-down menu. There is a search box on the left hand side of the 'Group Directory' page where you can search by keywords, category or language.

Once you have found a Group that interests you, apply to become a member. You may choose to send the Group Owner a message indicating why you would like to join—which is recommended as a matter of etiquette. The Group owner will review your request and usually you will have a response within 24 hours or so. When you have been accepted, a good strategy is to look at some of the discussions taking place within the group, how people respond and what value they bring to the conversation. Listen first and when you feel ready to step in and add something of value then speak up.

Important note: Some Groups have strict rules to protect their members from spamming or solicitation. Often this will be made known before you request to join the group and the Group administrators will banish those who break the rules from the Group.

Showing disrespect for the rules within Groups will also demonstrate to other LinkedIn users that you may have little respect for them in business, which may harm your reputation within the LinkedIn community.

139 The Secrets to Success on LinkedIn (. . . and other Social Media sites)

Social Media

Nathan Kievman, author of *Linked Strategies*, explains that the secret to success on LinkedIn is the philosophy behind using the site the right way verses the wrong way. The philosophy is that "You must always put your client's needs first".

Those who are there for their own agenda and not interested in helping others usually demonstrate that through their comments within Group posts or direct messages. Those who bring value to others usually do so through asking relevant questions; providing quality answers to questions posted by members; and reaching out to genuinely help others. By using this approach they often find they achieve their own outcomes as well—whether that be recognition, alliances with strategic partners, potential customers, recommendations etc.

Nathan Kievman even suggests you let people know how you can help them in your Profile Summary as well as noting what you may be looking for help with yourself. Just remember to update this regularly as your needs change.

140 Allow me to Recommend

Social Media

Recommendations are a great way to build relationships as it shows the person that you are writing the recommendation for that you care. When someone receives a Recommendation, LinkedIn automatically asks if they would like to return the favour.

Make sure that your Recommendation is truthful as it will only weaken your Profile if you are approached by another LinkedIn member to provide further information and you are unable to substantiate what you have written.

Make it a habit to send out a few Recommendations every week. Your Recommendations will show up on other members' Profiles and extending your visibility throughout the network.

141

Earn Expertise by Answering

Did you know that you can position yourself as an expert by answering questions asked by other LinkedIn members? When your answer has been selected as the best response by the person who asked the question, you gain a point of expertise in the question's category.

Where do you find the questions? Well, this time it isn't in the Group's Discussion area. Instead, go to 'More . . .' on the LinkedIn navigation bar and in the drop-down box select 'Answers'. There you will have two options: 1. To Ask a Question, and 2. To Answer. Select 'Answer' and then on the right-hand side of the screen you can 'Browse' the categories which might fit your expertise. Once you have selected a category then you need to start searching through the Questions and select the ones you are best able to Answer. Remember you need to have a 'value-add' answer or a point of difference that other people may not have presented. The person who asked the Question will then choose the Answer they feel is the best, hence earning you (if selected) Expertise points.

Another benefit of contributing to this process is that you again raise your profile, and position yourself as a credible expert within the LinkedIn community.

Blogging

- **More than 133,000,000 blogs have been indexed by Technorati since 2002**
- 77% of Internet users read blogs according to Universal McCann
- **Two-thirds of Bloggers are male (come on ladies, let's step up here)**
- One in five Bloggers report updating on a daily basis
- The most common rate of updating is 2-3 times per week
- Bloggers participate in an average of 5 activities to drive traffic to their blogs
- **56% of Corporate Bloggers say that their blog has helped their company establish a position as a thought leader in their industry**
- 58% say they are better known in their industry because of their blog

142   What is a Blog?

Social Media

Originally called *web log* the term has since been blended to *blog.* Blogs are a type of website that is updated regularly with commentary, pictures or images or videos. Most blogs allow interaction with visitors, giving them the option to leave a comment opening up a two-way dialog between the person writing the content and the person reading the content.

Since 2002, Technorati (http://technorati.com) a blog search engine, has indexed well over 130 million blogs covering topics from business to recipes. Blogging initially started out like an online journal but has now evolved into an online social media commentary. As blogging has gained popularity and increasing notice, particularly its role in covering breaking news stories, it has had a massive impact on some mainstream newspaper corporations, sending a number of them to the wall.

Unlike websites with their confusing coding requiring website designers, blogs can be set up in just a matter of minutes. They can be either hosted for free or if you require a more corporate blog with your own domain name you will need to arrange a hosting setup.

Google's Blogger (www.blogger.com) and Wordpress (www.wordpress.com) both provide the option to create and host your blog for free. You can choose a range of templates to give your blog a personal touch or even create your own if you so desire using simple point and click choices. Both Blogger and Wordpress have full tutorials on how to set up and get started with your blog; you can visit their support sites at http://www.youtube.com/BloggerHelp and http://en.support.wordpress.com.

If you are looking at something more detailed and corporate then you may decide to have a blog customised and built for you by professionals.

143 Choosing a Topic

Social Media

Although a blog can be a place to journal random thoughts and ideas across a variety of subjects, you will generate more credibility with both people who read your blog as well as the search engines if you focus on a few specific genres.

Ideally your topic should be relevant to your business, product, service or industry and provide great up-to-date information that is relevant and valuable to your readers.

144

Creating or Sourcing Content

Content can include articles either written by you or by others, pictures, images or video.

Articles might include information on changes within your industry and how it will affect your customers; or hints and tips on how to use your product. You might even do a "How To" style video explaining the process in easy steps—great for those who learn visually!

One place to source articles is www.ezine.com, however there are many other article directories where you can legitimately use the articles within your blog, website, newsletters and so forth. Just remember when using other people's articles from these sources you must always include the reference link at the bottom of the article—check the terms and conditions before downloading them for use.

145

Link Your Blog to Your Social Media

Successful bloggers participate in an average of five activities to drive traffic to their blog, such as including a link to their blog from a Twitter post or Facebook status update or including a link to their blog on their LinkedIn profile (don't forget that you can insert a Blog Roll application within your profile on LinkedIn which is very easy and it will update your network automatically every time you post something new on your blog).

146 Consistency is Important

Social Media

The most common rate of updating a blog is two to three times per week with one in five bloggers updating on a daily basis. Regardless of how often you update each week, it is important that you maintain consistency as people who follow you will start to expect regular postings and they may lose interest if you become inconsistent.

Consistency is also important in your message. Try to stay within your topic. If your business develops a new product that falls within a vastly different topic genre, then build a new blog that is focussed on that product and its industry-related areas.

Search engines such as Google pay attention to the number of posts you make; how regularly you post (i.e. twice a week or twice a fortnight); the relevancy of the information to those searching; and the quality of the links you post on your blog such as a YouTube video. This means you also need to be consistent in the keywords and phrases you use in all your content, in your tags or categories that you file those posts into on your blog, as well as the keywords used in the description of YouTube videos you might post onto your blog.

147 A Few Words of Warning . . .

Social Media

Social media, if used correctly, can be a very powerful medium to promote your message, your product launch, your services and your brand. But if you do not have a strategy in place first, you might do more harm than good to your business. Even global companies have found themselves in hot water by not addressing issues correctly only to incur the wrath of people following them on social media.

So before plunging into social media, decide what your social media strategy will be, what are your goals or outcomes, and how you will achieve them. Global giant, The Coca Cola Company, made their social media policies completely transparent by posting them on their website. You can view them at http://www.thecoca-colacompany.com/socialmedia/ where I am sure you will find some great tips on how to approach your online marketing.

Summary

Social media is changing the way we communicate our marketing message. Users who engage with businesses via social media expect complete transparency with those businesses.

Building a social media profile and following is time consuming and businesses need to have clear goals and strategies in place to achieve their desired outcomes. To save time it is best to use an aggregator type program that will allow you to manage all of your social media accounts from one platform such as www.hootsuite.com or www.seesmic.com.

Take time to respond to comments, both positive and negative and take the opportunity to demonstrate your customer service by resolving any negative issues openly. If you are afraid of getting feedback, then you perhaps should address this issue prior to marketing your business via social media.

Always give good value when posting content—share your expertise to the community by giving hints and tips in your posts on Facebook, Twitter or LinkedIn, add a 'how to' video on YouTube and link it to your blog and Facebook page. Post comments within

Groups or answer questions in the Answers section of LinkedIn to position 'you' as the expert in that topic.

Consider social media in the way in which you would consider attending a friend's party—you get the opportunity to meet new people, discover what they do, share a little about yourself and what you do but it would be considered rude to try to sell your products to the other guests.

Instead you would make an appointment to meet them at another time after the party. In social media terms you would invite them to visit your website where they can have the opportunity of seeing your product or service in more detail with the option to purchase if they desire.

Ensure your social media accounts are optimized for the search engines by having your keywords or phrases included in:

- The name of the Facebook page and the Info page
- Facebook mini-bio (underneath the logo area)
- Twitter Bio
- LinkedIn profile, summary and speciality areas
- YouTube information and each video's description (include your URL too)
- Blog title, description, categories (see an expert if you are unsure)

Each of these accounts can be ranked individually on the front pages of the search engines, giving you more exposure for your business. Your website will also benefit from increased rankings if it is linked to each of your social media accounts as the search engines will look favourably on these links.

Social media can deliver exceptional results for your marketing dollar allowing your business to be promoted not just locally but on a global platform opening up opportunities to build your customer database, sell products, open up joint-venture opportunities and much more. The secret to success is engaging people to your message. As Brian Solis says "Keep it Significant and Shareable."

Staff & Recruitment

"Asking questions will get you the performance you are after far better than dictating demands".

—Dan James

INTRODUCTION TO STAFF & RECRUITMENT

When I say I have over a dozen staff, some people look at me as if to say "are you a fool?". Having a team is a great thing, if you select the right team, and train and guide them well. Do it wrong, and yes, I can assure you, you will be living a nightmare. Remember that you are only one person, and you have only 24 hours in a day. With my team, I have 288 hours in a day!

148 Opposites

Staff & Recruitment

Yes, I know, you are the perfect boss. All your staff love you and you always do the right thing by them. Here are some tips on how to keep your staff happy and keep them in your business for a good period of time, so that your staff turnover rate is very low.

1. Give work (which has to be completed today) to staff at 4pm. Your staff love working in your business, and welcome every opportunity to work late and avoid going home on time.

2. If you know the deadline is say 3pm that day, let the material sit on your desk and give it to them as close to the deadline as possible. Your staff will appreciate the thrill of a tight deadline.

3. When giving business receipts to your Bookkeeper or Administrator, scrunch them all up into tiny balls so that they have to un-scrunch each receipt one by one. It's a relaxing task to help them unwind throughout the day.

(And I do know a fellow who did this; he said I was being paid to un-scrunch. The problem was that he didn't own the business and therefore didn't care he was wasting the bosses money).

4. Your staff will always welcome every chance to develop their problem solving skills, so withhold bits of relevant information or necessary documents.

5. Leave cheque butts and deposit receipts blank. Staff think of this as a fun little puzzle that they can test their skills on.

6. When your staff are away from their desk, feel free to use their desk, leave a mess or remove an important file. They will enjoy clearing up or playing "search and seek" for that file. It keeps them busy and makes their day go quickly.

7. If you have access to petty cash, borrow $50 from it, but don't tell the person who is responsible for balancing it. He or she thoroughly enjoys the mental stimulus of balancing the tin without knowing money was borrowed. (And yes, another true story. A business owner I worked for used to take money out of petty cash without telling me or leaving a note. I would reconcile and re-reconcile two and three times, panic that I was $50 short and then go to the boss, almost in a total state of panic to admit I had lost $50, only to discover he had helped himself. At this stage $50 was about half my wage . . . some years ago. I eventually took the key off him, even though he was the senior partner of the business).

8. Never thank your staff for their hard work and effort. After all, they are paid for their time; that is thanks enough.

As you would have guessed, this is really about what NOT to do. We all know the cost of recruiting and training a new team member is steep; so look after one of your greatest resources. Often a little thought, consideration and genuine praise for a job well done goes an awful long way.

149 What Motivates Staff to Work and Where

Staff & Recruitment

It is a statistical fact that staff's primary motivation is not money. Team members want:

- Job satisfaction
- Appreciation
- A sense of worth and value
- Feeling they are part of a team (hence calling them 'team members' versus 'staff')
- Opportunities for advancement
- Training and development opportunities.

So remember, it is not always about paying your team well, but about looking after them and valuing their contributions. Sometimes just a simple "thanks" or "shouting" them a pizza once in a while goes such a long way.

150 Be a Leader, not a Boss

Staff & Recruitment

It is a fact that you get more out of people from loyalty than fear. Yes, there are rules in place for a reason and there must be consequences if those rules are broken. However, being a tyrant type of boss will only mean your staff will follow you out of fear. Either fear of reprisal or being demoted or sacked. They will do what is absolutely necessary to stay out of trouble, but nothing more. They are not motivated to out perform or exceed your expectations.

However, the staff who have a great boss who is deserving of their respect and loyalty will naturally want to receive praise from their boss and will perform to the best of their ability. Why do people work? You probably say money, and yes, that is part of it, but there are many other factors that motivate someone to work for you—it may be challenge, enjoyment, mental stimulus, people contact, self improvement and more. There are people who work because they want to and not because they have to—so money is not the main motivator. Be a leader; treat people (especially your staff) with respect and courtesy and learn what motivates them and is important to them. Maybe performing well and being challenged is really important. If this is the case, then giving them interesting tasks and praising them when they get it right is exactly what they need and want. Also be sure to lead by example; if you expect your staff to not steal, then it is hardly appropriate that they see you 'rip off' a customer or supplier. Staff are very much like children in some ways—you teach them by example and they will follow your lead, so be sure you are leading them in the way in which you want them to behave.

151 Recruit the Right Person for the Job

Staff & Recruitment

In small business, you sometimes do not have the time, resources or energy to recruit properly. You don't screen, test, interview . . . it is just so time consuming. So, the first person who comes along who appears half capable, is given the job. It might be your sister, who has limited skills and experience, and is desperately seeking work. Fine, you might help her out—but do not give her the Financial Controller job at $80K per annum. Perhaps she is better suited to be an Administrator on $40K per annum (if she is prepared to do the training and fulfil the job needs). Remember, replacing someone later is very time intensive and money expensive. You not only have to recruit someone, but you also have to train them. You lose time in productivity, or your own time (or that of another staff member) and the person often is not productive for some time. Instead, invest the time now wisely, or if you really cannot do it yourself, outsource to a recruitment agency. If you are recruiting yourself, be sure to:

- Fully advertise the job, clearly outlining responsibilities, benefits and salary.
- Review all resumes received and make notes as you go.
- Reference check. Ring referees and ask lots of questions
- Interview the person. Not just a quick ten minutes (unless you know instantly that they are definitely unsuitable).
- Test the person. For example, if they say they can type at 80 wpm or know MYOB accounting software, then have them prove it. Remember, they are there to get the job and often will tell a prospective employer what they think you want to know. Discovering the truth afterwards can be costly in additional training you did not budget for.
- Involve a second person in a second interview. Often they will have a different perspective that can help you see more clearly whether or not this person will suit the role.
- Make a decision promptly. The 'good ones' will go quickly, so procrastinating may mean you are left with a second or third choice candidate.

152 Praise and Reward when it is Due

Staff & Recruitment

When a staff member does something incorrectly, we often are quite happy to tell them so. And that's fine, as long as it is delivered in a constructive and positive way, so they can learn from their mistakes. When was the last time that someone said to you 'great job'? How did you feel? Even a simple thank you takes almost no time or effort but it means a lot to many people. A quick one-line email to a staff member who achieved a good outcome, will work wonders. You will make them feel they are part of a team and that you did notice (and appreciate) their achievement. Even better, send the email to the whole team (if you don't have 100 staff) or make an announcement at a staff meeting. It is so nice to have our hard work appreciated and acknowledged. Yes, they are being paid for their work, but be realistic—if they put in a huge effort (above and beyond what is necessary) and achieve a great result and the boss/owner does not say a word—then they will ask themselves 'why bother in future?'

If you want those regular successes and extra effort exerted, then *you* make the effort and acknowledge them. How do you like to be treated? Treat others in this way. If you are not such a 'feelings' type person, then you may have to work harder in this department as it might not come naturally to you—but the extra effort will pay off.

153 Give Constructive Criticism

Staff & Recruitment

When someone does well, we praise them and likewise when they make a mistake, it may be suitable to correct them. If you know it is just a simple, once-off mistake, then no response may be required. If it is a major or recurring issue, then talk to your staff member, or supplier for that matter. You do not have to rant or rave; just point out what was wrong, try to ascertain why it happened and then work to find a way to ensure it does not happen again. Your emphasis should not be on 'rousing' but on future improvement. Maybe there is a system which is not working well and needs to be revamped? Maybe the staff member was not trained properly and needs further training. Maybe they were not given the right information? How can this be rectified in future? Work together with them to get it right in future. Or, if you know they simply didn't try, or didn't listen or didn't care enough to bother to do it right, then address this also. Remind them of what should happen, document the discussion and follow up to ensure it is on track a short time later. If not, you may have to 'discuss' this again. Always document such discussions, especially if it potentially may lead to dismissal, but always give the person the opportunity to improve, especially if they have the right attitude and want to get it right. If their attitude is wrong, then you may have to cut your losses sooner rather than later. I believe skills and knowledge can be taught; attitude is somewhat harder to teach.

154 Do not Bring Negative Moods into your Business

Staff & Recruitment

Just because you are the boss it is no excuse to behave poorly. Even if a staff member had a bad morning at home, you would expect them to turn up to work, cheerful and ready to work their full day. You don't want them to be moody or argumentative or worse, to abuse a customer because, for example, they are having problems at home. Well, it works the other way too. Do not bring your home life into your business, even if you are home based. You might be having an avid discussion (to put it nicely) with your teenager in the kitchen, and then walk into the office. The same tone should not be used on your staff. Even if you have to stop at the door and take five deep breaths, or go to the bathroom and count to one hundred, when you enter the office you should be in business mode. Be prepared mentally to be cheerful, bright and energised to have a full and productive day.

155

Respect Those Around You

Staff & Recruitment

I have worked in the building industry where colourful expletives were somewhat the norm, especially in a predominantly male environment. Just remember it is a workplace and using the "f" word or having posters of naked girls in the lunchroom or as computer screen savers really is not acceptable. Now, you may say to your female staff "toughen up" but be aware that if a staff member (male or female) found they could not work in your workplace due to these situations, you could find yourself being sued by that ex-employee. Do not put yourself or your business in jeopardy and just remember to do what is appropriate and expect the same from your staff.

156

Do not Fight in Front of the "kids"!

Staff & Recruitment

If you are a parent, you know it is bad to fight in front of the kids, but it amazes me how many business owner couples fight in front of their staff. And if you work with your partner or husband or wife, then do not have heated discussions in front of your staff. I can tell you—they absolutely hate it. Be professional or do it somewhere else. It might be wise, if you are a husband and wife team and you know you have a tendency to disagree, that you segregate duties. One person is in charge of finance and another in charge of sales. Or go out to a coffee shop for a weekly meeting to vent your disagreements. I have been in the middle of training couples and have had to sit there and witness arguments or even worse, one partner degrading the other—it is enough to make you quit. And never, ever, try to draw staff into 'taking sides'. Do not force your good staff to quit because you cannot behave in a professional manner.

157 Be Flexible Where at all Possible

Staff & Recruitment

Another drawcard to get and keep good staff is to be flexible. Some situations or positions may not allow it, but where it is workable for the business, allow a degree of flexibility. I have found there are some excellent parents in the workforce who have so much skill or ability, but due to family commitments can be limited in what they do. If you can offer school hours, or the flexibility to do some work at home, or even job sharing, then you can tap into this pool of excellent workers who will very much appreciate an employer who understands their needs and is able to help meet those needs.

158 Have a Letter of Appointment for all Staff

Staff & Recruitment

When you recruit for a position, you should have a list of duties that the position encompasses. Likewise, you should have a letter of appointment, or better yet, an Employment Agreement which outlines confidentiality, instant dismissal, pay conditions, accruals, benefits, rules, regulations etc. Ideally an Employment Agreement should be looked over by a solicitor, as it is a legal document. This document not only protects you, and your business but it actually protects your team. If it is clear that staff cannot take your ideas and clients and set up in competition with you, then this protects both your business and the team you have working for you. If your business is protected, it is more likely to flourish and in return, your team are more likely to retain their jobs. If one of the team quits and steals half of your clients, this jeopardises the jobs of other staff members. And to be honest, I think most staff like having these things in writing. They know what is expected from them, what the rules are (up front) and what they can expect from you. It is honest, open and transparent. We all know the rules and therefore can participate in the game in a fair and equitable manner.

159 Workplace Health and Safety is Important—Do not Ignore it

Even if you only employ one staff member, you must provide a safe working environment. The department of Workplace Health & Safety has excellent information and booklets to assist you. You may only have an office environment, where you think it is not necessary, but if you do not have a policy, education process and are diligent, you may find yourself with injured staff taking time off work, using up sick leave, or worse suing you. You may think that many WH&S issues are common sense. They are, but will a junior possess and use the same common sense you do? Will some staff take shortcuts because it is easier?

Never assume anything when it comes to the safety and wellbeing of your staff. Not only is it your responsibility to have a policy but also to enforce it. Imagine you have a policy regarding using safety goggles and you also ensure all staff have a pair, but one staff member refuses to wear them. If he or she had an accident, *you* the business owner are responsible. It is too bad they refused to wear the safety glasses; it is your job to ENSURE they do, or remove them from the workplace. It does not seem fair at times, but it is the law so be diligent.

Time Management

"The bad news is that time flies. The good news is that you are the pilot".

—Michael Altshuler

"Lost time is never found again"

—Benjamin Franklin (Inventor)

INTRODUCTION TO TIME MANAGEMENT

This is so true. You cannot get back time. You can't bank it up for another day. Once a moment has passed, it has gone. So many of us say we are "time starved" or "soooo busy" and yet, why is it that some people (even high up in large companies) do not seem to be rushed or panicked about time? Every one of us has the same amount of hours in a day, so what is the difference?

160 What is Time Management?

Time Management

What is 'time management'? Simply put it is being organised and efficient with your time. Time is something you cannot bank and you cannot get back once it is gone. You either use it or lose it. One of the most common complaints of a business owner and operator is that they are time starved, or time poor. Hey, we have all felt that stress of not having enough time. There are exactly 1,440 minutes in a day—every day. You use about 1/3 of this time sleeping which leaves about 960 minutes. Factor in eating, time with family or friends, travelling, showering etc and you are down to even less minutes left in the day. So use this time efficiently and effectively. The three main principles of time management are:

- Delete tasks
- Create shortcuts to do tasks more quickly
- Delegate tasks

161

Identify your Times Stealers

Give some thought to where **you** lose time. Each person is different and once you can identify where your time disappears to, then you can look at tackling that particular issue or issues. Here's a list to get you thinking:

- Interruptions—telephone
- Interruptions—personal visitors
- Meetings
- Tasks you should have delegated
- Procrastination and indecision
- Perfectionism
- Acting with incomplete information
- Dealing with team members
- Crisis management (fire fighting)
- Unclear communication
- Inadequate technical knowledge
- Unclear objectives and priorities
- Lack of planning
- Stress and fatigue
- Inability to say "No"
- Desk management and personal disorganisation

162

Establish Good Works Habits . . .
Brief Tip Summary Points

- Handle what you can, as soon as it comes in (but don't forget to prioritise)
- Start your day with the most difficult tasks first, or the ones you enjoy the least

- Create time for important projects by coming in a little early (but avoid staying late)
- To get a project started, select a start up task
- Start keeping track of how long things take
- Set time limits on projects and do not allocate more time to a project than it is worth
- Have a priority list and work on them sequentially
- Select jobs based on time available and have little jobs ready to fill in gaps or idle moments.
- Expect emergencies and interruptions
- Have a clock or timer available
- Take regular breaks, as being fresh will make you more productive.

163 Everything does not have to be 100% Perfect

Time Management

For the perfectionists out there—this is for you. Quite often 99% perfect is more than enough. Spending another 20% of your time on something to achieve that last 1% is often just not worth it. One example (one of my faults) . . . I will send an email, say to a staff member, and spend ten minutes writing the email (at which point it is 99% right), and then another five minutes formatting, tidying it, re-reading it and basically wasting time on making it 100% perfect. It does not have to be. We are not talking about putting together quotation for a new client. If you are a perfectionist (or OCD) then ask yourself—is the extra time really warranted? Is "near enough" actually good enough in this instance? Remember every minute you "waste" on perfectionism, is time lost; you cannot get it back and so cannot use it on something more worthwhile, like speaking with a prospective new client.

164 'Near enough' is not Always Good Enough

Time Management

For those who read the item above and realised immediately I wasn't remotely talking about you and you have the "she'll be right mate" attitude; then you probably need a dose of perfectionism. Remember that what you produce is a reflection of you and your business. Make sure your spell-check is turned on and use it.

Double check figures; at regular intervals I have seen balance sheets (where A is supposed to equal B exactly) come out not balanced. You send the message that accuracy is not important and that your service may not be "top shelf". Take that extra moment, to ensure things are right, accurate, correct and that what you say is included, actually is. If you know you are not great at spelling or grammar, consider using the services of a professional proof reader or editor, especially where the material will be seen by lots of people, such as with your web site. Now you might wonder why this is in time management. The reason is that doing something right the first time always is far quicker than having to rectify, fix or revisit to repair. So whilst you might take an extra few minutes to complete a task correctly now, if it saves you an hour then it's good time management—not to mention good business sense, as you might also be saving your reputation or retaining the business of a valued client.

165 Delegate! Delegate! Delegate!

Time Management

We all say how time starved we are and that we have "no time" but the fact remains that many small business owners have not fully developed the art of delegation. Yes of course we have all used the excuse "no one can do it as well as I do" or "by the time I show them, I could have done it myself". Yes, you are right on both counts; however this attitude will ensure you are forever working in the business and not 'on the business'. You will be forever a technician or worker and never a manager. Your business growth will be limited by the number of hours in your day and you will eventually burn yourself out. Learning to delegate can be a challenge for many, but done properly, it can work very well. You need to:

- Write a list of the tasks you do regularly. Then really look at each item in the list. Seriously, are you the only person who can chase up your debtors? Could someone else do the invoicing or put the newly delivered stock away? Below is a list of things you can delegate:

    - Easy or simple tasks which a junior or beginner could do (e.g. photocopying)
    - Non creative, repetitive tasks done on a regular basis (washing dishes, faxing, assembling packets, interviewing perspective employees)
    - Special projects or once-off or infrequently done jobs (trade show or proofing a book)
    - Tasks you are not proficient at, and that someone else can do better (e.g. bookkeeping)
    - Tasks you do not enjoy (such as cleaning or maybe debt collection)
    - Tasks that deplete you of energy or the time you need for more important activities

- Now, armed with your list of tasks you can delegate, consider to whom they can be delegated. Who is the best person for the job:

    - delegate to an expert
    - delegate to an equal
    - delegate to a beginner

Now, remember, even if you do not have staff, there are definitely tasks which can be delegated. Bookkeeping is a perfect example. Chances are you hate this chore, you aren't that good at it, it takes you away from doing what you do well (your business) and it takes so much time you end up staying up until midnight to "do the books". The smallest business can delegate this out to a contracted professional bookkeeper. Many work on an hourly basis; if you need two hours a month or four hours a week—they are flexible and you often only pay for the time used—the hours can increase or decrease in alignment with your business.

- Once you delegate a task to a person, you need to train them how to do the task (unless of course it is the professional bookkeeper who has come to you strongly recommended). I strongly suggest you have a Corporate Policies document which says how major tasks are done. If you have someone debt collecting, how often does it occur? Have the "Final Notice" template letters been written?

How do they track who they have called and when? What is the policy regarding follow-up? Do not just assume the person will know how you want this done, or will necessarily know how to do this well. Set procedures leave little room for ambiguity and it is great having the processes in place for when you have to train the next person—the training time is reduced substantially when there are pre-written support notes and instructions.

- Closely monitor the recently delegated task. Ensure the person is proceeding as desired and if not, provide further training or guidance (plus positive support).
- Empower your staff. If they do not have the authority to do anything, then you will spend an awful lot of time in supervising them and "holding their hand". Additionally, they will become disenchanted and feel you do not trust them.

- Regularly review and evaluate their progress with brief update reports so that you don't lose touch with what is happening in your business. Give them feedback or additional training if it's not quite right and keep reviewing, but pull back more as you can see it is consistently being done correctly.

166 Do What you do do Well— Outsource the rest

Time Management

I have mentioned this before, but I will say it again. You may be an excellent sales person, great electrician, wonderful designer, fabulous chef, dedicated doctor and you may well be able to do many other tasks but should you? You might have the intelligence or skills to do the task, but if for example, you are a doctor, should you be doing something like typing or debt collecting? An administrator's hourly rate is most likely going to be far less than your charge-out rate. What could you achieve in this time? Other tasks you may outsource, including marketing, cleaning, purchasing to name a few. There are businesses out there that do exactly this; virtual offices or corporate/personal concierge services.

167 Unpleasant Tasks

Time Management

If it is unsuitable to delegate these and you have to do them, then I suggest you:

- Get them over and done with first up in your day; allowing you the pleasure of hitting the tasks you enjoy
- Do not allow them to build up

- Ask for help
- Make the task more pleasant by listening to enjoyable music, or treat yourself to a chocolate. Even better, have the chocolate on your desk, waiting for when you have **done** the task—your reward.

168 Routine-ise and "Bulk up" Everything You Possibly Can

Time Management

One of the tricks to time management is to routine-ise as much as is possible. Some things in life are very repetitive, we do them day after day, week after week and invariably we do them exactly the same way each time. Other things you can do in bulk, so that instead of doing it several times a day or several times a week, you can be efficient and do it just the once. When I lived in a two-storey house, I regularly had to take things upstairs. So, when I came across something to go upstairs, I would place it on one of the bottom stairs. Later I would make one trip, and take up four or five things at once, instead of making four or five trips. Some things that you can re-utilise or bulk up, may be:

- Post a "Remember to Take" checklist by your front door.
- To simplify grocery shopping, meal planning, and preparation, come up with two or three weeks' worth of meals or even have a week 1, 2, 3 and 4 schedule of meals and use this month after month.
- Create a master shopping list and just print or photocopy it each week
- Set up your laundry space so that it includes all the items you need to do your laundry.
- Come up with a favourite wedding gift and baby gift, and designate these as gifts you will give every time you need a wedding or baby gift.

- Buy all your greeting cards for the year ahead at one time.
- Set up a bill-paying centre in your home wherever you like to pay the bills.
- Set up automatic payments for bills you pay every month.
- If you can afford it, hire someone to do the cleaning and even shopping
- Make a master travel checklist—a list of things to remember to pack or do before going
- Keep a toiletries bag pre-packed with duplicate soap, toothpaste, toothbrushes, etc. (Apply the same principle with the baby bag if you have young children.)
- Create computer templates for all the documents you find yourself typing over and over, such as emails, marketing letters, tenders and quotes. Anything repetitive; even the email you send to someone after meeting them for the first time.
- Make meals in bulk such as lasagne, spaghetti bolognaise, curry.
- Make up promo kits etc a couple of dozen at a time.

169   Reduce Interruptions—Set Times

Time Management

Operating in a business which is time based, I am really aware of the interruption factor in my work day because we do track time closely. Whether you work from home or in a formal office, the interruption factor can be devastating. Imagine you are working on a report and then someone pops their head in your door to discuss the weekend. You chat, losing direct time, but don't forget you also lose more time, as you then will need several minutes to re-focus on what you were doing before the interruption.

Plan your day and ensure that those around you are aware of your schedule. If people need to see you, they should not simply "drop in". Encourage co-workers (and even your staff) to book time with you—not just drop in as they feel like it. Book them all in a block. That way, they know they have limited time and the next one is waiting. Another trick is to book this time just before lunch or just before finishing time—most visitors will keep it quick to avoid cutting into their own personal time. At home, have work time and family time. Communicate this clearly with your family and stick to it! If children know you work until 4pm and then will come out and spend time with them, they will learn to wait, but be prepared; pens down at 4pm sharp! I know personally I get engrossed in what I do, so put an alarm on your mobile phone to go off five minutes before your deadline.

170 Reduce Interruptions—Furniture & Comfort

Time Management

Whilst it is good to have a comfortable chair for your clients, this is not a good idea to have in your office. If room allows, have a boardroom where you meet clients and in your office avoid the comfy chair—so as not to encourage the "stay arounds". This also has a dual affect; if your meeting room is separate, your meeting will not be interrupted by your office phone.

If you are in an open-plan office, position your desk and chair (if possible) so it is not facing others or facing the door. This way you can eliminate some of the impromptu interruptions through easy eye contact.

171 Reduce Interruptions—E-mail

Time Management

We all have it. We all love it and hate it. Email can be great to save you time; it avoids the ten minutes of idle chatter of a phone call, you can just get to the point and say what needs to be said.

However, the amount of emails we get inundated with can be a time killer.

Firstly, I strongly suggest you know how to touch type. We all spend so much time emailing, if you are a one or two finger typist, you will never get past more than about 40 words a minute. If you type 80 plus words a minute you are naturally going to get things done in half the time. Do a typing course; the investment of your time will be well worthwhile.

When you email, be succinct, do not prattle on and say clearly what you want. If you have a number of questions, ask them all at once. This means you might get back only one email, not ten responses to the ten emails you sent. Internally, teach your staff email procedures. One thing we have is a NRR code. This means 'no response required'. It might be I'm telling a staff member something, but I want to just say it and move on . . . not have it going back and forth.

Decide when it is going to be quicker to pick up the phone. Sometimes ten emails back and forth are just not worthwhile; a quick ten-minute call may wind up the matter, especially if it is a complicated matter.

Do not use email for sensitive matters. As it is in bad form to break up a relationship via email or text, it is the same in business. Do not terminate the services of a long-term supplier via email, or strongly reprimand a staff member, or worse, sack them via email. Have the courage to do these unpleasant tasks either face to face, or if necessary over the phone. It avoids the angry emails back and forth. Never write an email (and send it) when you are feeling angry or emotional. If you must write (to vent) be sure to stick it in your drafts folder. Dealing with the hostile email response can not only be time consuming but emotionally draining.

When you email to make an appointment, include three time/day options and take the initiative to suggest a location or venue. This means the person responding only has to choose one of the three dates/times and accept the venue. If you spread out the dates, it is likely they can make one of the three and the appointment can be made and finalised in one email with one response. Confirm the appointment closer to the date with a quick email.

On some matters, you can give alternative names or contacts details for your staff if the person has any queries or difficulties. You can just tack on a note "if you need help restoring this file, just ring Mary or Jane in my office on xxxx and they will be able to help you over the phone". Essentially you are delegating.

Turn off the sound for your email application's "inward alert". It takes extreme discipline to not check your mail the second you hear that "beep". Again, allocate your time so as to do emails in a group—finish the task you are on and then check all the emails at once; perhaps once an hour or so.

Take yourself off junk mail lists or have a separate email address for these. I have two email inboxes; one for the business emails which I clear almost 24/7 and then another to which I have newsletters etc sent. Some of these I do need to read as they are informative and educational, but I tackle them at a time which suits me. Anything I don't really want, I will block.

Set up (or have your computer tech set up) your email so that spam emails go straight into a spam folder to avoid having to sift through these, but beware that an important email from a client does not end up in your "spam" folder.

172 Reduce Interruptions—Turn off the Phone

Time Management

Good business etiquette says you turn off your mobile phone when you are in a meeting, however I am amazed at how many business people do not follow this practice. A meeting cannot be successful if you are constantly excusing yourself to answer your mobile and it really does send a message to the other person that you don't think their time is of value. So, now I often pull out my mobile and turn if off in front of the person I'm meeting, and say something like "I'm just turning this off so we don't get any interruptions". Most people get the hint and follow in suit.

173 Reduce Interruptions—Batch

Time Management

If you have staff, encourage them to see you with batches of queries or requests. For example, a junior may need help but rather than approaching you 15 times in a single day with individual queries, request they hold on to them all and see you once with a batch of queries—then they can spend five minutes with you and get back to work. All staff, junior and senior should be taught the concept of "batching" to avoid multiple interruptions. Alternatively, encourage staff to query things with you via email—even if they work in the same room as you—I have found this does work out to be quicker for the simple stuff.

174

Reduce Interruptions—Use an iPod

In some circumstances—especially open plan offices, it is actually beneficial to allow staff to use an iPod or MP3 player. By having the earphones in, they can avoid background noise and the random interruption factor—it is like working in a private bubble. Personally, I find a snappy tune helps me to keep up the pace whilst working and I can easily avoid the "idle chatter" without appearing rude.

175

Reduce Interruptions—Hold the Phone!

Have a period of your day where you do not take phone calls; aim for your most productive part of the day. If you are a morning person and at your most efficient early in the day, advise your receptionist to tell callers you are "unavailable" until 11am. Yes, I realise this means you chance playing a game of "telephone tag" but the advantage of hitting the work hard for a couple of hours will outweigh the disadvantages. Just ensure your reception does not use the phrase "she's busy" as this sounds like "she's too busy for you". If you work at home, instead you may do as I do. I work from 4:30am to 7:30am and then stop to get my children ready for school, have breakfast, put on a load of washing etc. I get more done in those first three hours, than in an entire day. If you have a set routine, regular callers will get to know your patterns and just start automatically calling you after 11am. Also communicate this to your staff, so they don't have to waste time learning your pattern.

For calls you *never* want to take, such as telemarketers, train your staff/receptionist to screen properly or if you don't have staff then quickly interrupt and advise the caller you are not interested. I think some telemarketers have the ability to not breathe, so I wouldn't wait for them to pause or draw breath. Just jump in. As I have caller ID, if someone calling from a "private number" rings between 6-7pm, I often do not even answer the phone and let the answering machine screen for me, as it is a sure bet it will be someone soliciting for something.

176 Reduce Interruptions—Curve "Internal" Interruptions

Time Management

Internal interruptions can be time consuming too; being hungry, tired, thirsty etc, so here are some tips to offset those internal interruptions:

- Be organised and go to the toilet or get your coffee before you start
- Encourage coffee trip sharing with a co-worker, for example, it is far more time efficient if one of you makes two coffees at the same time; alternatively group your coffee trip with a toilet break.
- If you are tired, then have a coffee or coke (and ensure you get enough sleep at night!).
- Prepare snacks ahead of time and have these handy when your stomach starts to rumble.
- Have a water bottle on your desk for easy hydration.
- Have a planner or diary handy so that any random (but important) thoughts can be jotted down straight away, so you do not have to totally leave the task you are working on.

177 Conversation Enders

There are always people you just cannot wind up, especially on the phone: here are some beaut one liners to end a conversation:

- "I don't want to take too much more of your time . . ."
- "I know you're busy. I'll call you next week with the report . . ."
- "I'll let you get back to . . ."
- "Before we end this conversation . . ."
- "I've got to go now, but can we talk about this Friday when I see you?"
- "I've got to leave in five minutes. Can you sum up your last points?"
- "Just one more thing before we hang up . . ."
- Tone of voice that you're winding up with single words like "okay" "alright then", "great".

Don't forget meeting windups tips:

- Wear a watch and use it.
- Stick to the time you have allowed; even set that time with the person beforehand "so do you think 30 minutes will be about right?" so that this way, they also know the time limit.
- When you are ready to wind up, use that wind up tone, and start picking up your things or even suggest "I'll pay for the coffee" . . . all of these sort of things say it's time, and the meeting is over. Of course you can be direct and simply say "well, I've got to get to my next appointment, but it was great catching up . . ."

178 Attempting too Much

Time Management

I must confess, this is me! Many of us feel we have to accomplish everything yesterday and do not give ourselves enough time to do things properly. This leads to half-finished projects and no feeling of achievement. I personally take on too much and am often not realistic about how long something will take to do. Especially as a working mum, we tend to just take it all on and figure we will somehow juggle all the balls without dropping any. The problem is, often things can slip through the cracks. Perhaps it is a child feeling neglected, or a report sent out which was not proofed properly. Put realistic times on activities and do not attempt to do more than you know you reasonably can, factoring in a strong likelihood of interruptions.

179 Learn to say "No"!

Time Management

For some personality types I know this is really hard, but to be successful in business (and even in your personal life) you have to learn to say a firm but polite "no". Like telemarketers who hound us around dinnertime, some people just cannot take no for an answer and if they sense indecision or weakness, go in for the kill. When someone (and I am not referring to the Director or CEO of your company) asks you to do something, do not immediately response with a yes. Consider:

- Do I have the time to do this?
- Do I want to do this?
- Will it benefit me or my business?

For example, I do one charitable free bookkeeping service at a time. So if I am currently the treasurer of one, then I would decline anything further. However, once I had moved on from that position and if I wasn't doing anything, then I might consider something similar for another charity or community group.

Another classic is someone else delegating to you. Everyone from children to staff will try this. How many parents have had children try to lumber them with their homework? Staff and co-workers can be the same. As the boss, do not allow staff to not finish something properly before giving it back to you—ensure they have suitable training/instruction and then relegate it back to them with a clear instruction that they need to finish the task properly. If a co-worker tries it, and you are quite busy, just politely apologise and say you have a deadline to meet and will not be able to get it done.

If a client asks for something to be done within an unreasonable timeframe, then you have to consider a few points. Is this just a once off and not a normal pattern? Can you help them out this time, but be clear that in future you will need x days lead up time? If your client is consistently disorganised, can you anticipate your client's needs and chase them up well before the deadline so that you do not have the last minute panic?

At the end of the day, you may well consider this client not worth the stress and choose to cull them. A 'good' client isn't just one who pays their bill on time; they are often those who cause you the least stress.

180

Lack of Priorities/Objectives

Time Management

This is probably the biggest and most important time waster. It affects all we do both professionally and personally. Those who accomplish the most in a day know exactly what they want to accomplish. Unfortunately too many of us think that goals and objectives are yearly things and not daily considerations. This results in too much time spent on the minor things and not on the things that are important to our work and our lives. Try having a (short and reasonable) list of things you need to do today. Do this each morning before you start your day (or the night before) so that your day is reasonably planned and structured. List the items in order of priority and do the first thing first. Work off this list and try to not be distracted by other tasks which are low priority or which are time wasters. If you catch yourself being involved in an unproductive activity, stop it straight away. As you mark each task off your list, you will find it very satisfying. Even allow yourself rewards for achieving results.

You can incorporate a similar procedure with your month by anticipating what is going to happen and allowing time in advance. For example, we become very busy in the week leading up to a quarterly BAS deadline, so I always plan to not do much networking that week and even write into my diary "office" time where I block out chunks of time to ensure I stay in the office and do not book appointments.

181

De—clutter your Desk

When you have finished reading this chapter look at your desk. If you can see less than 80% of it then you are probably suffering from 'desk stress'. The most effective people work from clear desks. I know myself that a clear desk is a clear mind. Have an in-tray. Work from this tray and when you do something, have that item only on your desk. Complete it fully and then move it on. Then pull out the next item and work on it. I assure you that you will work more effectively.

182

Procrastination

Procrastination tends to be a personality trait. Some people are never procrastinators and others are always, or I find I procrastinate when I am not comfortable with the issue at hand and really don't want to accept it. I procrastinate, but instead I should just make the decision to say no or withdraw and be done with it. By avoiding making a decision you are wasting time. By reducing the amount of procrastinating you do you can substantially increase the amount of active time available to you and also to those around you. Having a boss or client who is a procrastinator is very frustrating. In this case, may I suggest that you make the decision for them, for example, by saying "I will organise this format of the business card on Monday, unless I hear from you otherwise before then". You have achieved a few things by doing this. You have shown initiative, taken away the need for them to decide, achieved a deadline, but still kept them informed and given them the opportunity to override.

Procrastination can occur when you:

- Feel uneasy—maybe you are indecisive because it is wrong. Recognise this and act.
- Are not ready—arrange to get all the bits together, so once you are prepared, you will be ready to start.
- Are feeling overwhelmed—break the task down into "bite size" pieces so it is manageable. Often doing the hardest part first allows you to get started and then you can proceed. Concentrate on one thing at a time.
- Hate the task—delegate it, or do it first and get it over and done with. Then, and only then allow yourself to do the tasks you love and enjoy.
- It is bad timing—know your unique personal rhythm and plan your schedule around it.
- Need pressure—if you work well under deadlines, set mini deadlines to achieve results along the way, or set yourself personal deadlines, which are actually days or hours before the actual deadline.

183 Meetings

Time Management

Many managers and business owners spend substantial hours in meetings. It might be with a Board, staff, suppliers or clients. Here are some practical tips for successful meetings:

- Have an Agenda for the meeting and circulate this before the meeting; that way participants can be prepared for the meeting. Make it known that any "new business" should be on the Agenda where possible (thus to avoid matters being raised which are not suitable). Have times allocated to each item. Send a reminder message that morning reminding participants that the meeting will be starting sharply on time.

- Have a strong Chairman or person to run the meeting. Someone who will stay on task, not allow rambling, disputes, arguments or drawn out discussions and debates. If there is no-one running the meeting, then take it over yourself and maintain the structure.
- Kick off on time. Close the door and make it clear that arriving late is not appreciated.
- Have a separate timekeeper if the person running the meeting is not as disciplined, that way, once the ten minutes allocated to the third item are used, it is time to either decide or re-table the matter and move on.
- Schedule meetings before lunch or just before "knock off" time so participants are not inclined to hang around and drag it out to avoid their work.
- Avoid having food and snacks at meetings, unless the meeting is being held at lunchtime. Settling in for a good munch is sure to not keep the pace moving.

184 Overcoming Chronic Lateness

Time Management

Work out why you are late? Every time you have been late, ask yourself why. When you judge how long it will take to get somewhere, do you estimate incorrectly? Do you not allow a little spare time for things like traffic, road detours or difficulties finding a parking spot? I suggest you always tack on 20% of the travel time for this purpose. If the trip is only down the road, you do not need to leave 15 minutes early, but if the trip is an hour away tacking on 15 minutes is very wise. You can always take out some reading to do if you do happen to make good time.

Do last minute distractions delay you from walking out the door? If so, this is a discipline point on your part. Do not take calls on your way out, tell your receptionist to inform the caller "he just walked out the door, but you might get him on his mobile". Then you will not be delayed AND you can handle the call whilst driving (using hands free and as long as it is not a call for which you need to take notes).

Do not try to just finish off that last thing before you go—if it is going to make you late. Allow time to prepare to leave; packing your briefcase, combing your hair, bathroom visit, finding your keys or actually getting down the lift to your car or the taxi.

Arriving on time is a choice—make the choice and do it. You will arrive de-stressed and ready to do business.

185 Multitasking

Time Management

Derived from the first sense, multitasking is the colloquial term for a human being's simultaneous handling of multiple tasks. "Polychronistic time" is the business jargon way of describing multitasking.

As good as people say they are at multitasking, I believe performance drops off, no matter how much mental energy is expended for two or more additional tasks done simultaneously. The mind gets tired. "Research suggests that the prefrontal cortex mediates a person's ability to depart temporarily from a main task in order to explore alternative tasks and then return back to where they left off. Performing several separate tasks consecutively is known as multitasking. This complex mental juggling comes at a price, however. Researchers measured a 20-30% loss in the total time it took for subjects to complete two separate problems, when they switched back and forth mentally between the tasks. A specific type of multitasking behaviour that plays a key role in human cognition is called branching, and depends on the front-most region of the brain, the anterior prefrontal cortex, an area especially well developed in humans compared to other primates.

Studies suggest that humans may be the only species capable of performing branching, which involves keeping a goal in mind over time (working memory), while at the same time being able to change focus among tasks (attention resource allocation)."—*Journal of Experimental Psychology: Human Perception and Performance*, August 2001.

On this basis, of the mind getting tired, certainly most of us cannot do multiple things well at once, but I have learnt as a mother of three that you can certainly mix some things. My own philosophy has been to do two or three simple things at once (such as load the dishwasher, stir the dinner and hear spelling from a child). None of these are brain teasers. Or have a medium-level task joined with something so simple you don't need to think (such as tidying your desk a little). But never attempt to do two high level tasks at once. For example, I would never talk to a prospective new client whilst typing something or replying to an email. For a start, I will sound vague as my focus is not 100% on that person and secondly they will hear my fingers clanking on the keyboard. My dad caught me out once doing exactly this!

Examples of multitasking:

- Clean your desk whilst on the phone—how hard is it to put pens in the drawer etc whilst having a conversation.
- Have handy a business magazine or newsletter to read when you expect to be kept waiting—such as when going to the dentist or an appointment with your accountant.

- Catch up with friends or family on the phone (hands free obviously) whilst peeling the spuds (or even better, delegate this to one of the kids . . . who is old enough to not shred his hands). It will not work with a business call as you may have to take notes and be that bit more focussed.
- Test spelling in the car taking the kids to school (but ensure siblings don't pipe up with the answers).
- Use doing household chores (such as sorting socks) with your kids to both get them to help you, but also it is a great opportunity for one-on-one time to talk with them.
- If you need to spend time with your staff, such as them asking you questions, do this whilst eating your lunch. You can listen to their questions and munch at the same time. Just ensure onions are not on the menu.
- Return calls in the car; but be selective. If you think you will need to take notes, then avoid those calls until later.

186 Analyse your Time

Time Management

Are you spending enough time on the projects which although may not be urgent now are the things you need to do to develop yourself or your career? This might be attending workshops, networking, or reading business journals. Are you constantly asking yourself "What is the most important use of my time, right now?" You should focus on 'important tasks' and stop reacting to tasks which seem urgent (or pleasant to do) but carry no importance towards your goals.

You should also know where you spend your time and possibly map out a schedule. Plan things for when you know you are most productive and also plan time for self development, family, and most importantly, YOU.

Below is a shell of a time planner sheet. You can write in, or just colour code activities.

	MON	TUES	WED	THURS	FRI	SAT	SUN
5am-6am							
6am-7am							
7am-8am							
8am-9am							
9am-10am							
10am-11am							
11am-12pm							
12pm-1pm							
1pm-2pm							
2pm-3pm							
3pm-4pm							
4pm-5pm							

187 Regularly Review

Time Management

Once you become a good time manager, don't forget to regularly review your practices and try to think of more or new ways of saving or utilising your time. And remember "there is always enough time for the important things" . . . make sure you allocate time to what is important to you in your life!

Work / Life Balance

"It's not what you do once in a while; it's what you do day in and day out that makes the difference".

—*Jenny Craig (Diet Guru)*

INTRODUCTION TO WORK / LIFE BALANCE

Owning and operating a business definitely equates to hard work, but it does not (and should not) mean you do not have a life. Believe it or not, you actually can have it all. The trick is to find the balance where work stops and your life kicks in.

When we initially start a business, this is definitely the time to devote a vast amount of time and energy; however you need to set a limit on how long this "start up phase" lasts. Ten years on you should not still be doing 18 hour days. I believe the first twelve months are full on. Then you should be able to cut back, say to 12 hours for the next year and then further cut back to what is a reasonable time for you.

What is reasonable for you? Well, that certainly depends on the other factors in your life. If you are like me and a single mum with three kids, then 30-35 hours a week may be your limit. Perhaps you don't have children, or they have "flown the coup", but you may have a partner, or aged parent—my point is this—make time for the other important things in your life.

188
Consciously Plan your Work/Life Balance

Work Life Balance

My first advice is to write down what is important to you. It might be family, spiritual belief, playing a sport, a hobby, reading, self improvement, charity work, making your home nice, gardening, surfing, partying . . . the list could go on and on. Once you have this list, put it in priority order.

Now once you have your list in order, allocate time to each of these activities per week. Remember you need to allow time for sleep (say 8 hrs x 7 days), time to eat, time to shower, cook, wash your clothes etc. Now factor in your work hours and see what is left. If you choose to work additional work hours, then what other time activities will you sacrifice? By doing it on paper, it is far more a conscious deed. What will you choose to not do in lieu of the extra work hours?

189 Ensure you do not Lose Sleep at Night

Work Life Balance

If you do not get enough sleep it will affect your mood, memory and concentration. You will be less productive and less able to concentrate or remember things. Lack of sleep makes you irritable and cranky, affecting social interaction and decision making. It will make your immune system vulnerable to infection and disease. And If you drive when seriously sleep deprived it is similar to driving while drunk. So, how do you get a good night sleep?

- Have no coffee/caffeine after mid afternoon; a minimum of four hours before bedtime.
- Do not use street drugs like Ecstasy, cocaine, amphetamines—they are stimulants, and like caffeine, will keep you awake, not to mention their main effects.
- Reduce the stress. Allowing yourself time to "think" during the day, and not at bed time, will more likely provide a solution to the problem that is causing you stress. Not every problem can be solved, or is within your control. In that case you need to allow yourself time to worry, and then accept you cannot do anything and file that "worry" away.
- Do the right thing. Honesty does allow you to sleep at night. Be truthful and you will not worry about unwanted repercussions.

- Stop work at a reasonable time and have mental leisure/ wind down time. Watch some TV, read a novel (not a technical journal, it will just put your brain back into gear), or do a crossword or puzzle.
- Exercise is a fantastic way to sleep well at night, but again, allow wind down time, so the adrenaline can stop pumping. Allow at least two hours wind-down time before bed.
- Have a shower or bath.
- Have a light snack or suitable drink. A glass of warm milk 15 minutes before going to bed will soothe your nervous system. Milk contains calcium, which works directly on jagged nerves to make them (and you) relax. Or have a cup of hot camomile, catnip, anise or fennel tea.
- Alcohol. Some people believe that a nightcap before bed will help them sleep but alcohol actually reduces your sleeping quality.
- Smoking causes sleep troubles in numerous ways. Nicotine is a stimulant, which disrupts sleep.
- Play calming music. There are CD's designed for that very purpose.
- Have your spouse give you a massage just before going to sleep. A short backrub or face rub or scalp massage can be a big help.
- Keep a note pad by your bed—use it to take notes to remove mind clutter. Once you write the note/idea down, then you know you can forget about it and clear your mind.
- Ensure your bedroom is completely darkened and quiet. If there is a party going on next door, use earplugs. Ensure the room is a comfortable temperature with adequate ventilation. Finally, ensure you have a firm and supportive mattress. Do not skimp here. How many hours a week do you spend in bed? Far more, I will bet, than you spend wearing your favourite pair of shoes or using your favourite golf clubs!
- Reserve your bed for sleeping, not working on your laptop, watching TV, paying bills or checking reports.

- Do not go to bed too early. Your body goes though cycles of alertness and drowsiness later in the afternoon. Also napping can interfere with sleep. If napping works for you, fine, but if you are not sleeping well at night, cut out that "nanna nap".
- If you cannot fall asleep within 20 minutes, get up and do something boring until you feel sleepy. Some relaxing techniques are:

  - Deep breathing. Close your eyes, and try taking deep, slow breaths, making each breath even deeper than the last.
  - Progressive muscle relaxation. Starting at your toes, tense all the muscles as tightly as you can, then completely relax. Work your way up from your feet to the top of your head.
  - Visualising a peaceful, restful place. Close your eyes, imagine a place or activity that is calming and peaceful. Concentrate on how relaxed this place or activity makes you feel.

- Finally, insomnia can be a symptom of a physical disorder, although for most of us it is the result of tension, stress and anxiety, so if you still cannot sleep, it might be wise to see your doctor.

190 Set Limits

Work Life Balance

Once you have worked out what is important to you and what you want to do and the priorities, then you need to set limits for yourself and be strong. For example, I do a fair bit of networking. For me, because my kids are all older and one of them is really an adult, it is easy for me to do breakfast functions. So I do these and sometimes a couple in a week. However, my personal rule is that I do not also do evening functions. I choose one or the other and then I am very firm with invitations (and myself) on what I accept. Yes, I do the occasional evening function, but I am VERY selective with those I attend and I definitely do not do both ends in one day, i.e. breakfast networking and evening networking. If you want to have a life, and have a family (who don't have to paste a photo of you on their wall to remember what you look like) then set your rules. To some people I just say I have a prior engagement that evening, to others (whom I know better) I am honest with them and explain that I do heaps of morning functions, and my evenings are reserved as "family time". No-one has come back to me yet and given me a hard time about this. I believe gone are the days when there was a perception that to be successful, you had to work 90 hours a week. In fact, you seem to be more respected now if you are successful AND have a life.

191 — Learn to say "NO"

Work Life Balance

Saying no is a really hard thing for many people. By nature, many of us want to say yes, especially if we can possibly manage something. Perhaps you are being asked to meet an unrealistic deadline, or just slip in an extra meeting. Maybe it is a simple question, like "can you find me the Smith report?". Be selective about what you say no to, but definitely think before you say yes. Ask yourself, do you really need to do this thing? Can you delegate it to someone else? An example could be a client rings and says "can you help me with restoring this file, it is just not working". Rather than me spending 20 minutes on the phone with that person, my answer is "Sure Mary, we can help you! I'm just going into a meeting, but Julie here will definitely be able to help you—I'll just pass you over to her". I have helped my client, but I've delegated the task to one of my team. Notice in this case, I didn't actually say "no" but in essence I did, I just had a different solution.

Sometimes it is a definite no. I have been asked to sit on committees and realised it just will take too much of my time. So I have thanked the person for considering me, and explained that if I take on something, I do it right, but I just know I'm pushed for time at present, so will decline. Nice but firm.

192 Avoid Crazy Deadlines

Work Life Balance

Again, with the concept of "no" is negotiating with people. Perhaps a client has said that they want something by Wednesday. This is going to put an enormous amount of pressure on you. But rather than saying no (because you don't want to), say to them that you would love to help them out, and keen to do the job, but Wednesday is going to be extremely difficult. What about Friday, could that work for them? It might be that they can quite well live with Friday and this takes a bit of the pressure off you. You can only ask—if you don't ask, then you don't know.

193 Avoid Stress Triggers

Work Life Balance

We all have stress triggers. Sometimes it is deadlines, or overwork, or a task which is hard, or traffic . . . the list goes on. Think about what your triggers are and then how you can avoid them. If running late stresses you, then allow extra time to get to an appointment. This was one of my own triggers, so now I always add ten minutes allowance to the journey. So if I am running a little late, no stress, I still arrive on time. Perhaps heavy traffic frustrates you? Then avoid appointments during peak traffic times to reduce your stress. If your bank reconciliations cause you an endless amount of stress, then delegate this task. Only you know what stresses you, so take a step back and see how you can avoid these triggers.

194 Remove the Clutter

Work Life Balance

For me, a messy working environment does not make me productive. If the office is neat and tidy, and my desk cleared, then I think much better. Remove the clutter (get someone to come in and clean) and then you can focus on what is important and not stress about the piles of things you need to action or need to put away.

195 Relax

Work Life Balance

If you do find yourself stressed, stop and take a few deep breaths. Better yet, get up and go for a walk (even if it's only to the toilet) or change tasks and do something pleasant, before returning to this task. If you can take a longer walk, take the dog and circle the local park. You will definitely come back feeling refreshed.

196 Exercise

Work Life Balance

Do not say you are too busy to exercise. Like everything else you do, such as business planning, networking etc, you need to build this time into your schedule. Actually write exercise activities into your diary, such as gym, golf, fitness class, footy etc. If it is in the diary, it is more likely to be done and less likely to be "bumped" for a work activity.

197 Eat Well

I am no dietician, but if you are living on take-away, fast food, fatty or greasy foods, then you are filling your body with the lowest quality fuel. Just like your car performs better on premium fuel, so your body performs better on quality nourishment. Eat regularly, consistently and well, and you will feel better for it. If you feel better, then you work better. Remember fresh food is always better than pre-packaged snacks. And try to drink two litres of water every day. Have the water bottle on your desk and empty it daily.

198 Do not Overburden your Schedule

We all try to put way too much into our day. We have back-to-back meetings and projects to work on and then of course need time for admin, emails and returning phone calls and wonder why we do not achieve everything in our day? Or worse, keep working in the evening in order to try and catch up. Be realistic with your time. Do not over-schedule yourself, but instead, spread out your meetings and have quiet times in your diary purely to catch up.

199 Anticipate Time Snatchers

Again, part of the over-burden concept; allow time for activities which take up our time. On any day you know you are going to receive a certain number of phone calls, or emails and you know one of your team is going to need time to talk to you—so plan this when scheduling your time. If you know you need three hours a day for these sorts of admin tasks, then do not book out your diary for full days—otherwise when are you going to fit in these "time snatchers"? Not all of them can be delegated or avoided.

200 Book a Holiday

Work Life Balance

This is a good one for me. I get caught up, then realise it is Christmas, and go to book something and everything is taken, or now a ridiculous price. Plan your year in advance and book regular holidays. If you decide you will have a week off in late January, a week at Easter and then a week in late September, why not (a) book it in your diary and (b) actually make the booking and pay your deposit. Having booked and paid, and blanked out the time in your diary, it is pretty much assured you will follow through on having that break—and come back to work re-charged and ready to conquer the world.

But read on . . . you get three extra tips for free.

201 Live (and operate your business) Within your Budget

Work Life Balance

One thing that stresses many people is cashflow, or rather, the lack thereof. Just as we should have a budget and "live within our means" as individuals, so we should do the same for our business. If your business cannot afford $10K on advertising each month, then change your marketing process, so that you are not spending big bucks and replace with other activities instead. Not maxing out your credit card and having enough money in the bank for wages will probably go a long way to help you to avoid finance-related stress. But to do this right, you need to have a budget.

202 Have Quiet or Think Time

Just as you schedule time for meetings, admin etc, you should be scheduling quiet time, or time to think. I know some business owners, who take a whole day off, get away (maybe hit the beach) and just think with a note pad. Maybe it could be just an hour in the garden. My two best thinking places are in the shower and in the car driving—that is when I get my best ideas, so often when I am in the car, I will not actually return phone calls—instead it is just a quiet time to think.

203 Laugh

Work does not have to be boring, tedious or depressing. Have a laugh, read positive affirmations, read the occasional funny email. Maybe subscribing to a "joke a day" email might just be the way to start your day. Maybe it's about surrounding yourself with people who love life and whilst they work hard, also believe in having a bit of fun along the way.

In Conclusion . . .

I hope you have really picked up some valuable tips here. Business is about making money and succeeding, but I strongly believe you can love what you do and have some fun along the way. I also believe in learning from others' mistakes and others' successes. Why re-invent the wheel?

Use the ideas in this book and pluck out the concepts and strategies which you believe can work in your business to go out there and give it your best. By reading this book, you have taken the first step to business success. Congratulations!

Author Biography

Donna Stone has been bookkeeping for over 25 years and a MYOB Consultant for over 16 years, as well as having run a Private Employment Agency for three years. She has worked in top legal and accounting firms, as well as operating her own successful business *Stone Consulting* for over 10 years which now has over a dozen staff. Whilst she does have formal qualifications (Advanced Diploma of Accounting, Cert IV Workplace Trainer & Assessor and Cert IV in Small Business Management, plus she is a Registered BAS Agent); it's the years and years of real world experience that has made her into an industry expert she is today.

Donna currently has professional memberships with:

- National Institute of Accountants
- Institute of Certified Bookkeepers
- Associate of Accounting Technicians—Fellow
- Australian Institute of Management—member over 25 years
- Australian Society of Authors
- Queensland Writers Association.

In addition, Donna has won a number of Business Awards, including being a National Finalist twice for Small Business Champion, won Queensland state awards twice and a number of local awards—mostly in the category of 'Professional Services'. She was also awarded "Networker of the Year" in 2010 and has been involved in a number of business networking groups, including holding the position of 'Education Officer'. Donna is also a single mum of 3 boys (or rather young men now) and actually finds (some) time for sport, hobbies and one or two other interests.

Having helped numerous clients, and with all the above experience, Donna believes she has the experience, skills and knowledge to share—helping other businesses succeed. *Stepping Stones to Business Success* is the first book in the *Stepping Stone* series, which aims to help businesses succeed, grow and ultimately excel. The series will include:

Stepping Stones to Business Success
Stepping Stones to Business Growth
Stepping Stones to Business Excellence

Whilst Donna is not new to writing, and has in fact had dozens and dozens of articles published in various business magazines, including *My Business Magazine* and *Working Women Magazine,* this is her first printed solo book. One which she is very excited about. She has been the guest writer as an industry expert for Glenn Walford's book *Maximising Your Franchise.* A business associate recently said to her "Well about time you decided to share all that info in your head with the rest of us!"

Would you like to know more, or contact the author? Please visit our website www.donna-stone.com.au or email the author at donna@donna-stone.com.au. The website includes the latest on speaking engagements and what's happening, testimonials and heaps of great free material.

Donna is always open to feedback and would love to hear about anything specific you would like covered in her upcoming books—it's all about you and what you want to read.

And finally, some special thanks to:

Julie Mason—my wonderful guest writer, who so kindly shared her great expertise and knowledge of Social Media—a massive thank you for your input and time. You really are the Social Media guru.

Tracey Tolley—my assistant, who has dealt so well with all the tasks I have given her; both in the business, but also in assisting me with this book. She's handled everything from setup, structure, systems for book orders, the website, and so much more.

Wendy Smith (Jewell See Editing)—my Editor—for your valuable input to this book as well of course all the proofing you performed and suggestions you made.

Saul Edmonds (Roundhouse)—my cover artwork designer. I knew what I wanted and he was able to convert that idea from my head to paper. Thanks for making it happen.

To my wonderful endorsers; all of whom were more than happy to read the sample chapter, but also gave me such glowing endorsements and testimonials.

To my great network of business associates and friends—you are all awesome!

And finally a huge thank you to YOU. Not only did you buy this book, but you took the time to read it. I do *hope* you have read it and didn't just skip to the back page! I greatly appreciate your support in reading this and sincerely trust you have picked up many great tips—to help your business not only succeed, but to help you personally succeed in whatever you endeavour.